# Paintings & Poems

by Diane Barron

ISBN: 978-1-879628-57-1

Published in association with Keokee Books., in the United States of America.

Front cover image by Diane Barron.

www.keokee.com

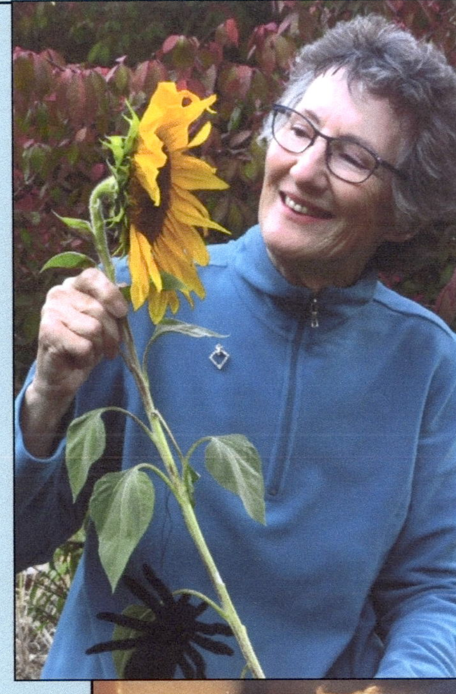

# Paintings and Poems

Though I've always liked to have fun with words, the acrylic paintings came first. It is here there are hours upon hours of effort. Long before this combination jelled, I had a welcome critic say, "Your paintings are like poems." Perhaps this planted the seed. Do they need explanations?  I hope not.  Are they open to interpretation?  I hope so.
It's all pretty personal, but I don't take myself too seriously.  My thoughts aren't unique.

Categories are flexible.  Most of the old houses were farm houses. Many paintings have an oversized flower, which symbolizes continuation. Most of the paintings are done from photos I have taken while on road trips. I've taken the liberty to include some photographs.

I have done many things, but my career was teaching high school art. I reside in North Idaho  with my husband, Don, and three cats.  With admiration and love I dedicate this book to Don, not the cats, and to sons Neil (Kara) and Jay (Thuy).

*We are what we repeatedly do.*
*Excellence then, is not an act, but a habit.*
*-- Aristotle*

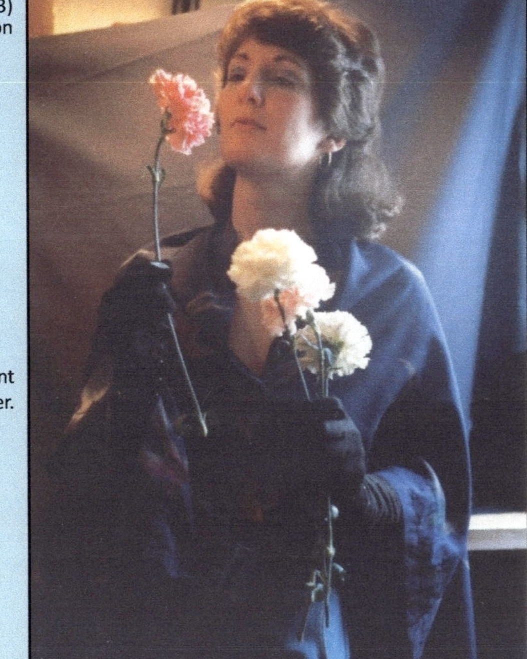

Photo (1983)
by Don Barron

I am an excellent
house cleaner.

# 1. Of Roads & Waters

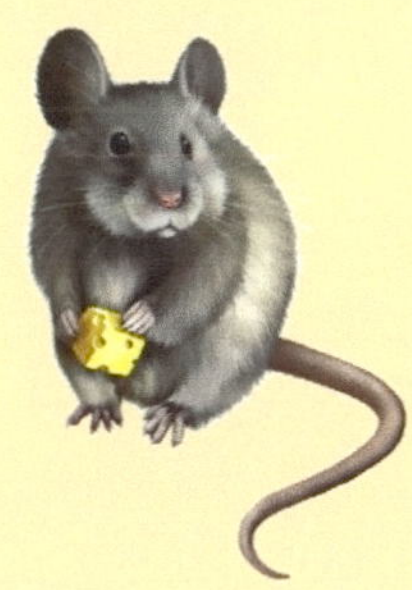

## Mouse in the RV

It's nothing fancy...our Class C RV,
but it's neat and tidy and fits to a T.
Midnight camped along the river,
skittering sounds gave me a quiver.
The motion light flashed by the sink.
I had to do a double blink.
There on the counter in silhouette,
a mouse was doing a pirouette.
Around the counter he did run,
I think he wanted out...not fun.
On the floor, across the table,
he was growing quite unstable.

Up the wall to the over-cab bed,
where my husband lay his sleeping head.
Down again to who knows where,
I can't rest...can only stare.
Like a mummy all tucked tightly,
I finally fell to snoring lightly.
Morning was too suddenly there,
but smells of coffee filled the air.
I hope to never repeat this night,
not that it was a terrible fright.
I think I've found a solution for that.
Now we travel with a cat.

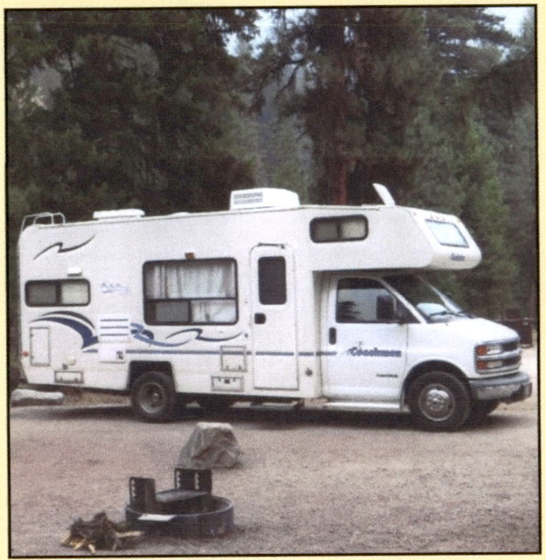

# Drumroll on the Au Sable

If by good fortune you catch it right,

you'll see an unforgettable sight,

of majesty and might.

Repetitive by nature's clock,

far below sheer walls of rock;

from 100' above the river

colossal chunks of ice do quiver,

pushing the jagged mass downriver.

Intensity it does deliver;

opening warmer springtime waters

to those who view like spellbound
squatters.

Drumroll sound…low vibrating rumble,

crash of symbols as they tumble;

layered in a piled-up ram,

deep they sink in a turquoise jam.

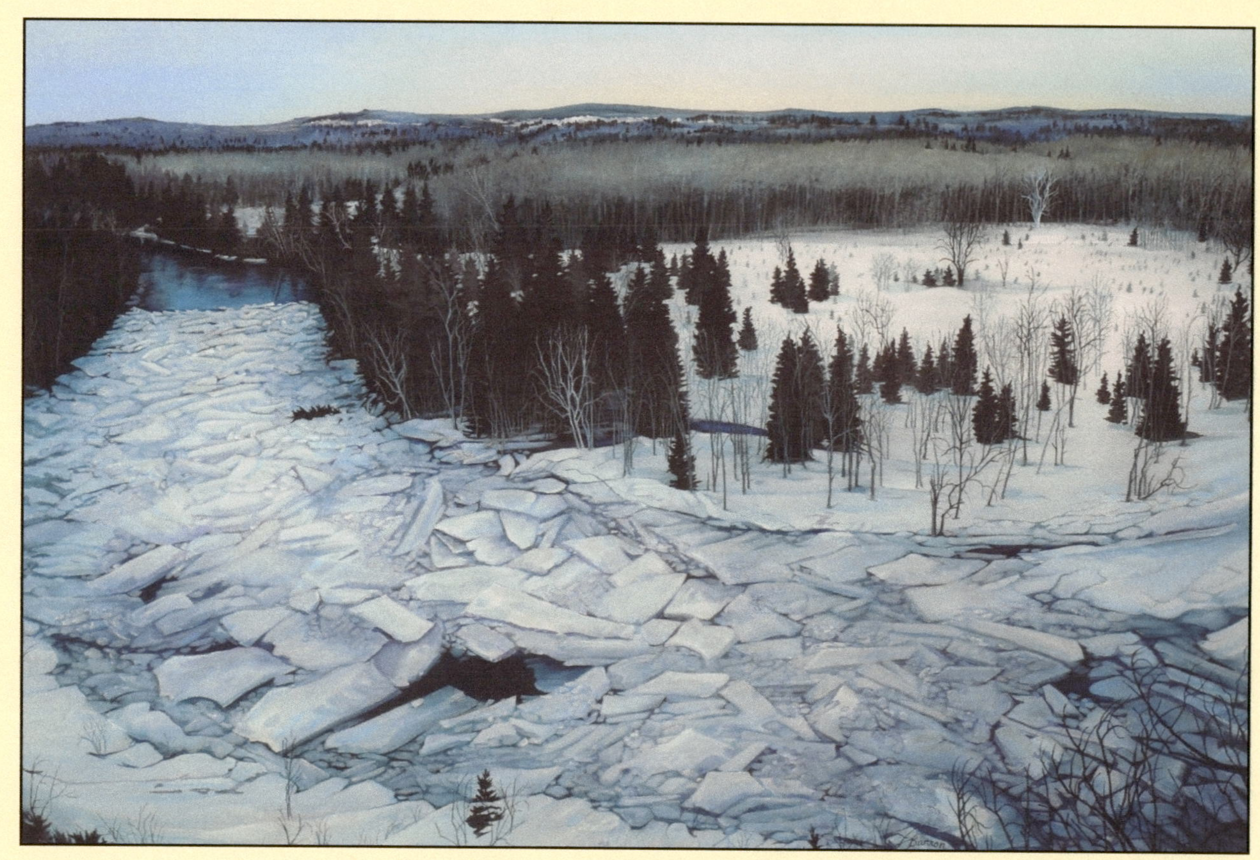

**Drumroll on the Au Sable** | Cover Art, Highbanks Overlook, from a 1977 photo

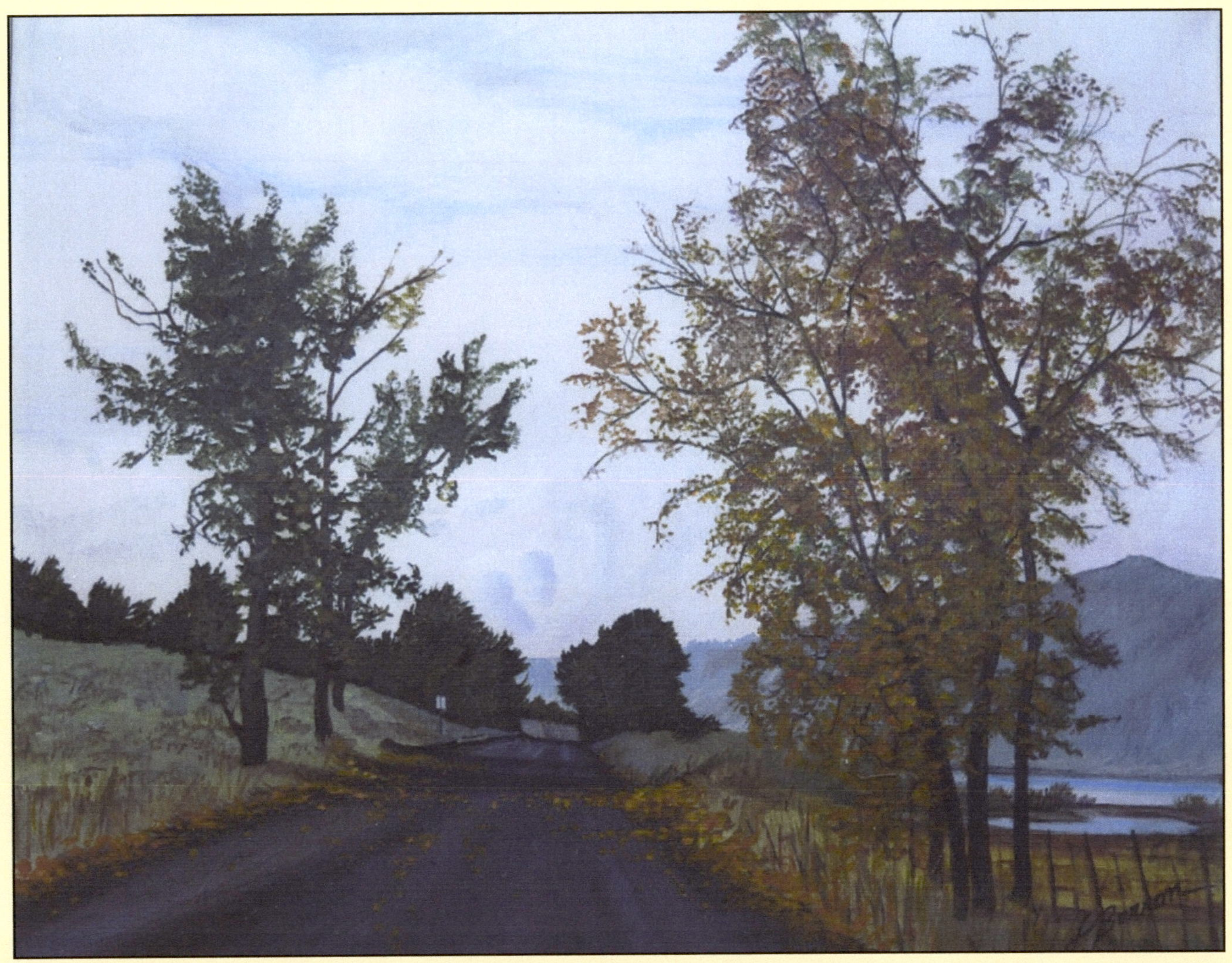

**Cemetry Road**

# On the Road

We're ready for some days to slip,
all packed up for a little road trip.
Willy crooning *On the Road Again*;
some places we have already been.

Country roads and vistas grand,
stunning sights...some are bland.
Husband is the driver steady,
slim relief when he is ready.

Small town diner our interest piques,
where lucky we will find antiques.
Two lanes are just fine with us,
keeping it simple...don't like fuss.

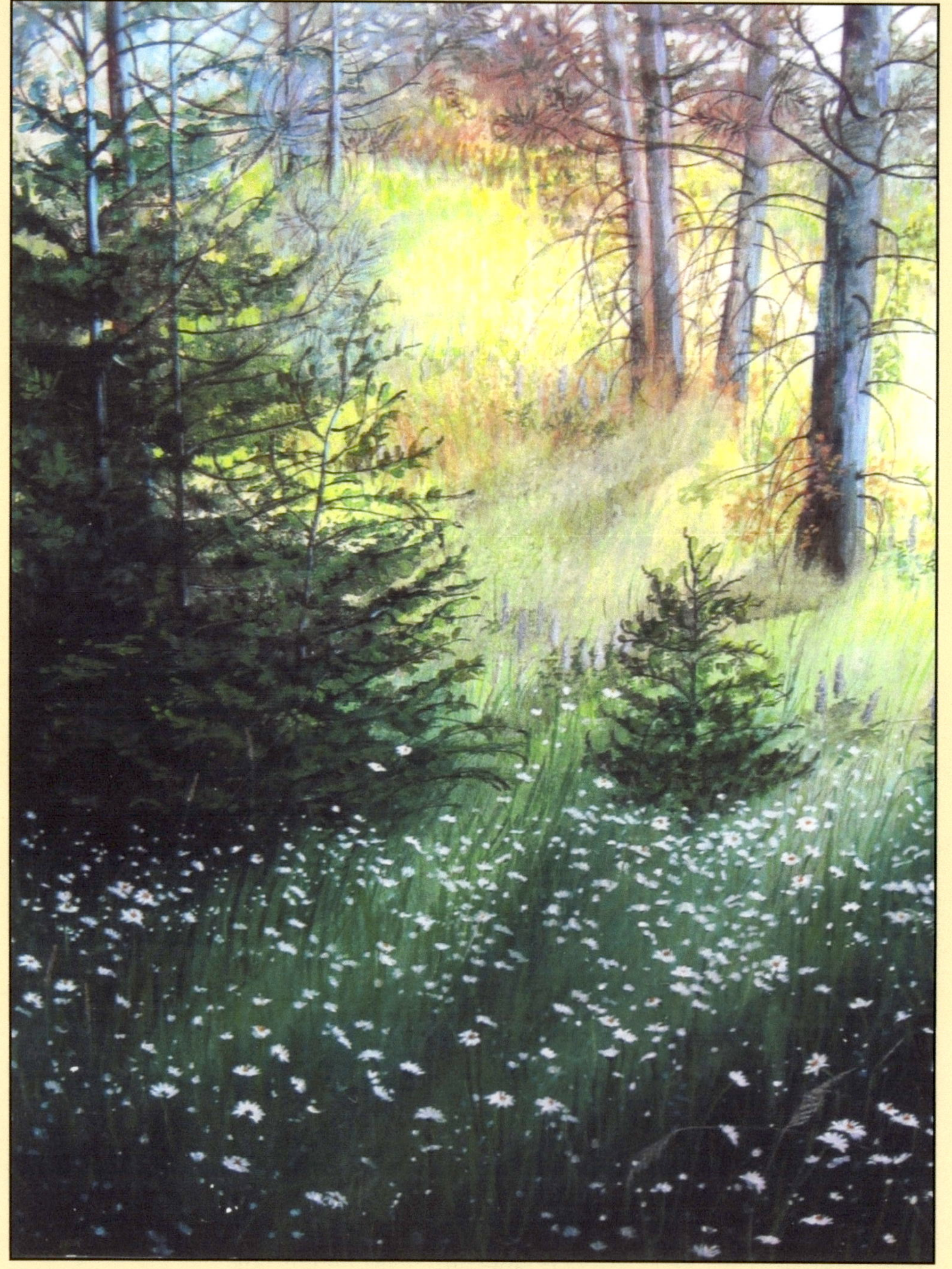

**Meadow Gift**

# Meadow Gift

Wild daisies are in bloom,

like carpet in an outdoor room.

They grace the meadow like a gift,

give your mood an instant lift.

Butterflies land and flutter in play,

bows upon this nature wrapped day.

No returns...no need to pay;

a special delivery each late May.

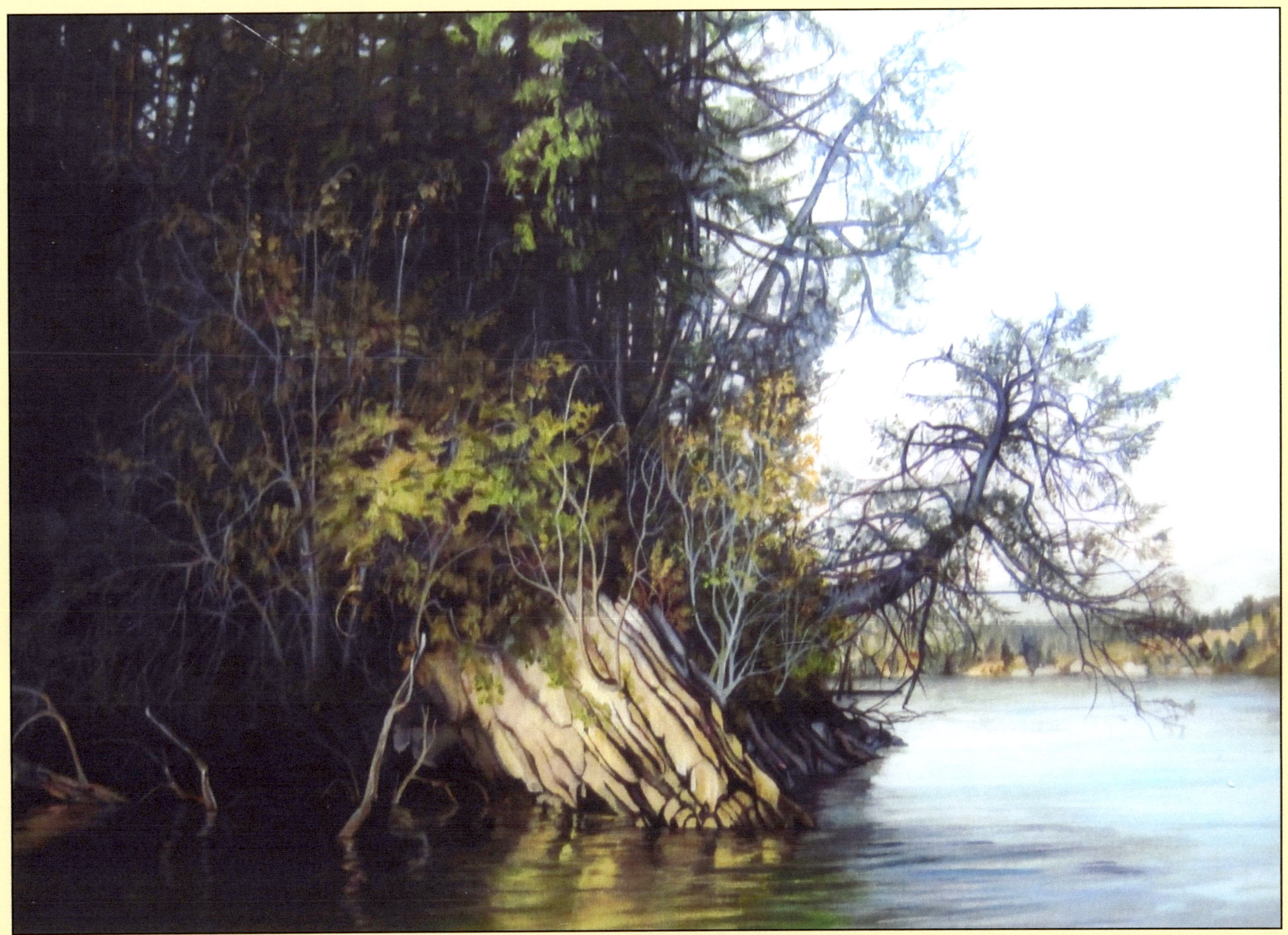

October, Coeur d'Alene Lake

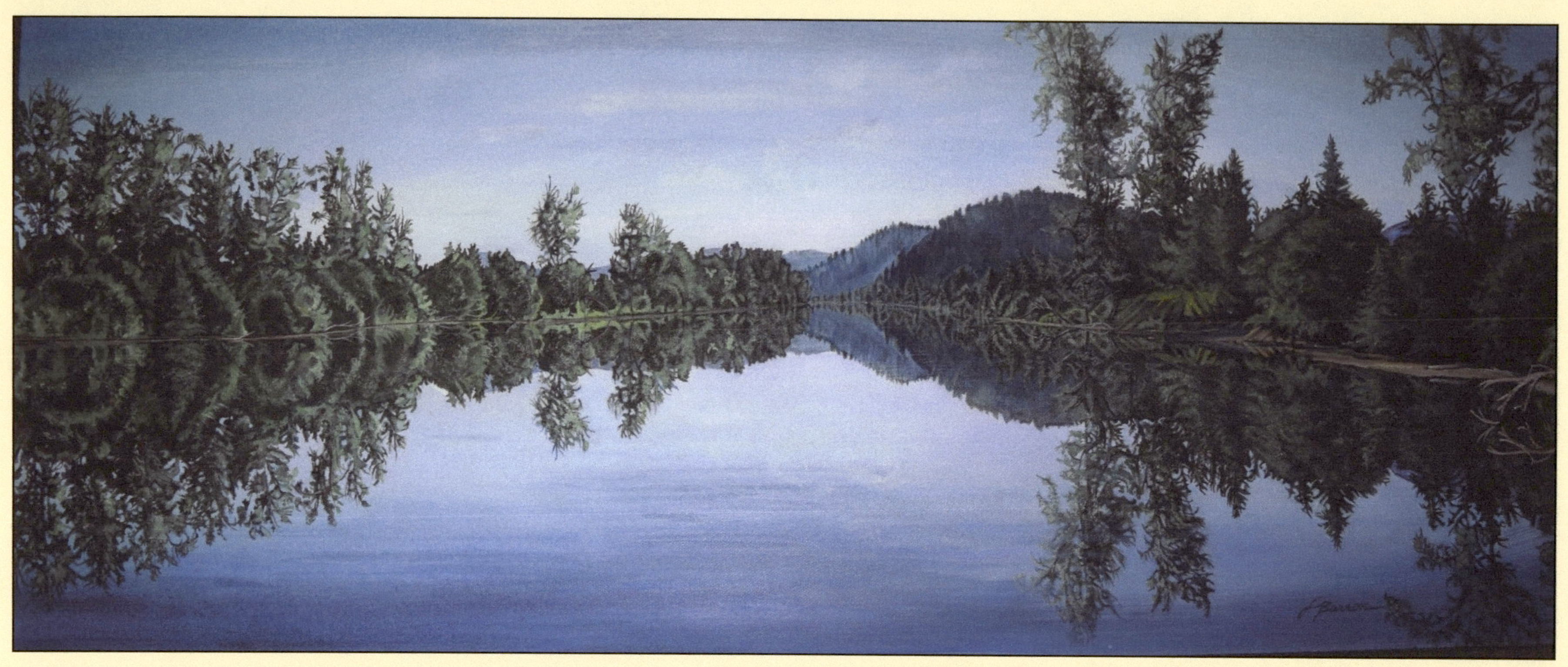

**Double Down the St. Joe**

# Double Down the St. Joe

A kaleidoscope of shapes

above the amber shoreline drapes;

as foliage doubles on each side

varying in how tall and wide.

One view up...the same view down,

mirrored in the dark blue gown.

Tranquil waters carry the eye

to the vanishing point where earth meets sky.

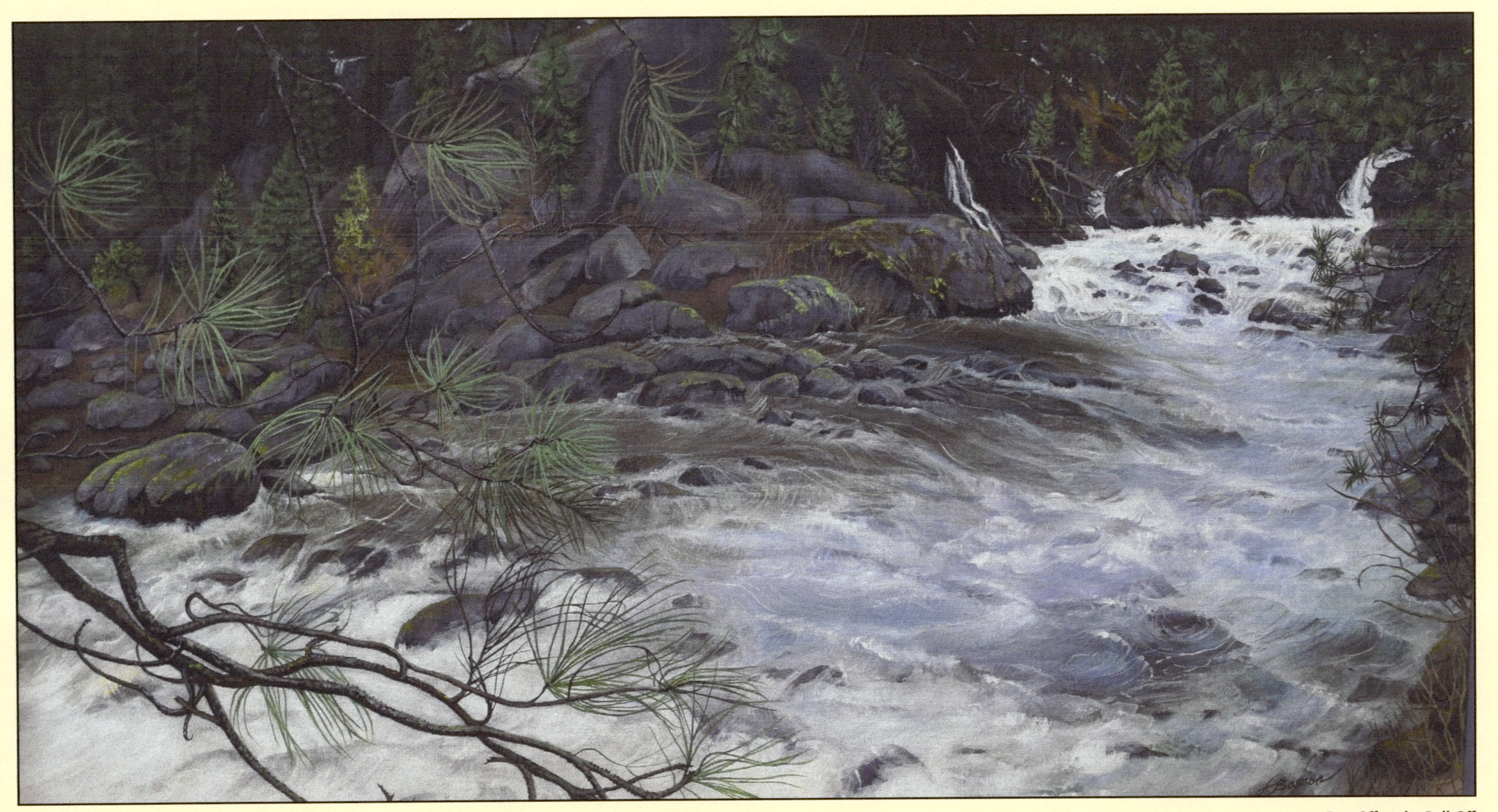

Run-Off at the Pull-Off

# Oceans Away

An ocean is a mysterious thing,

crashing waves or shimmering bling.

Repetitive movements mesmerize;

far water blends with hazy skies.

Fishermen labor to feed the world,

even though they're tossed and hurled.

Darkness in the depths unfathomable,

plants, fish…creatures unimaginable.

Expeditions to faraway shores;

mermaids, Selkies…old folklores.

Surfboarding and pleasure boating,

paddling or just beach floating…

I much prefer to stay on land,

finding shells…toes in the sand.

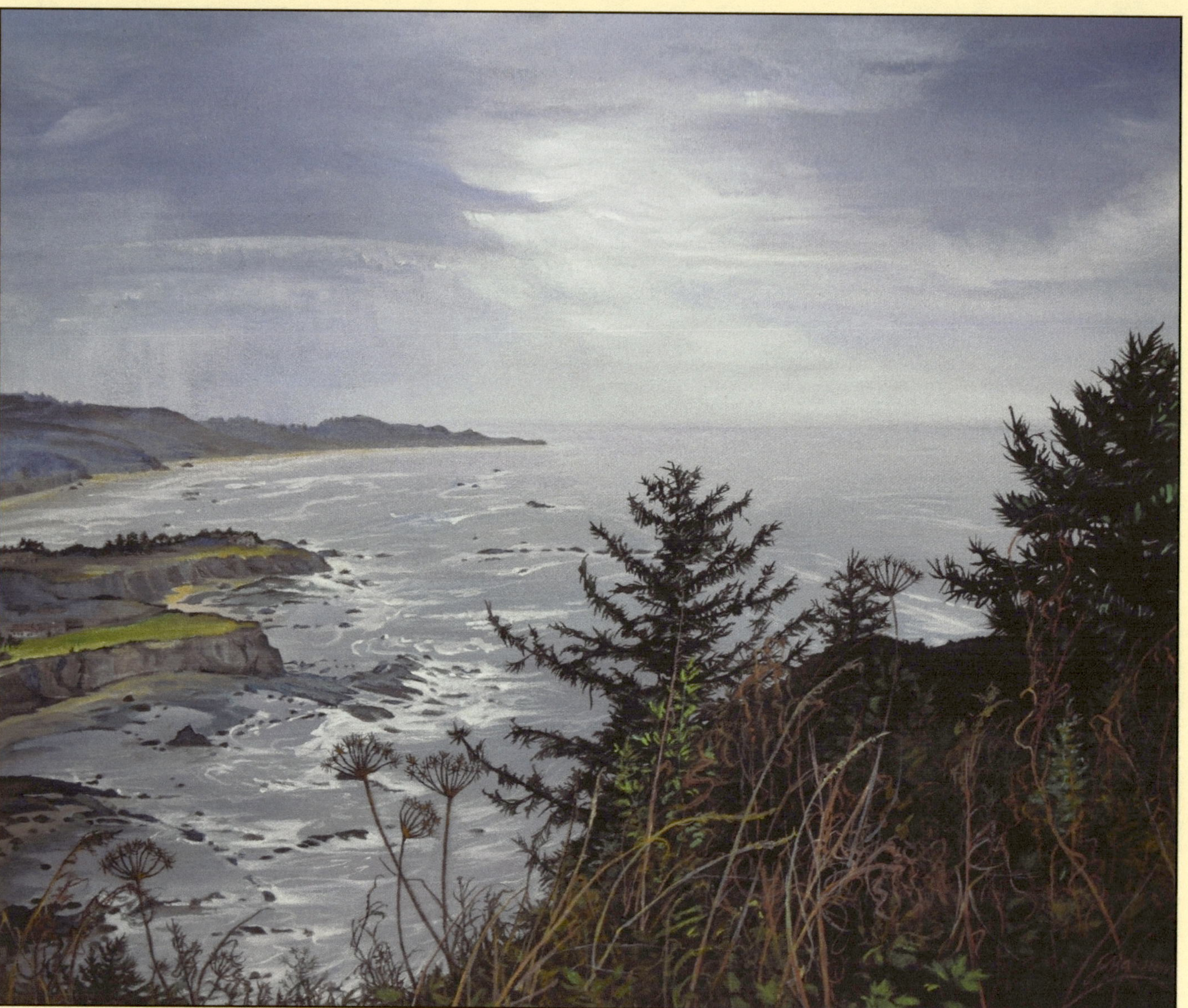

Oregon Overlook

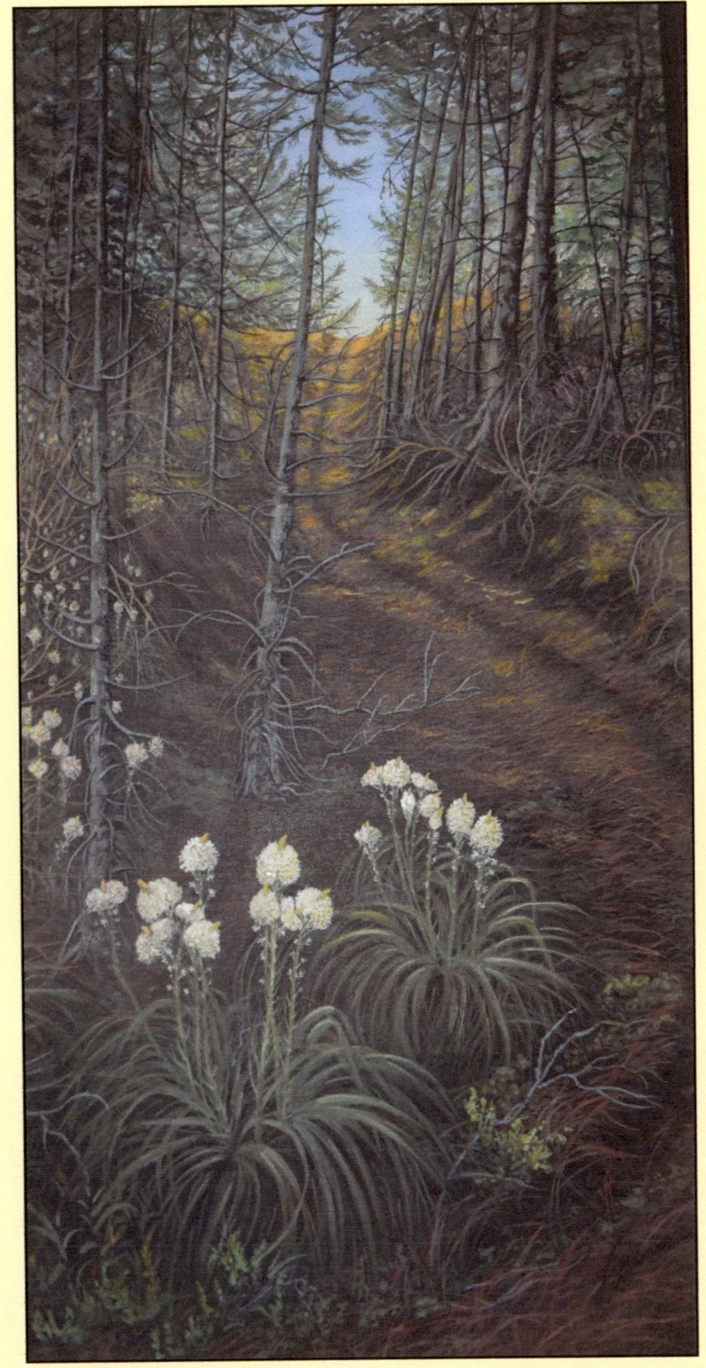

Bear-grass at the Pass

Mom's Millpond

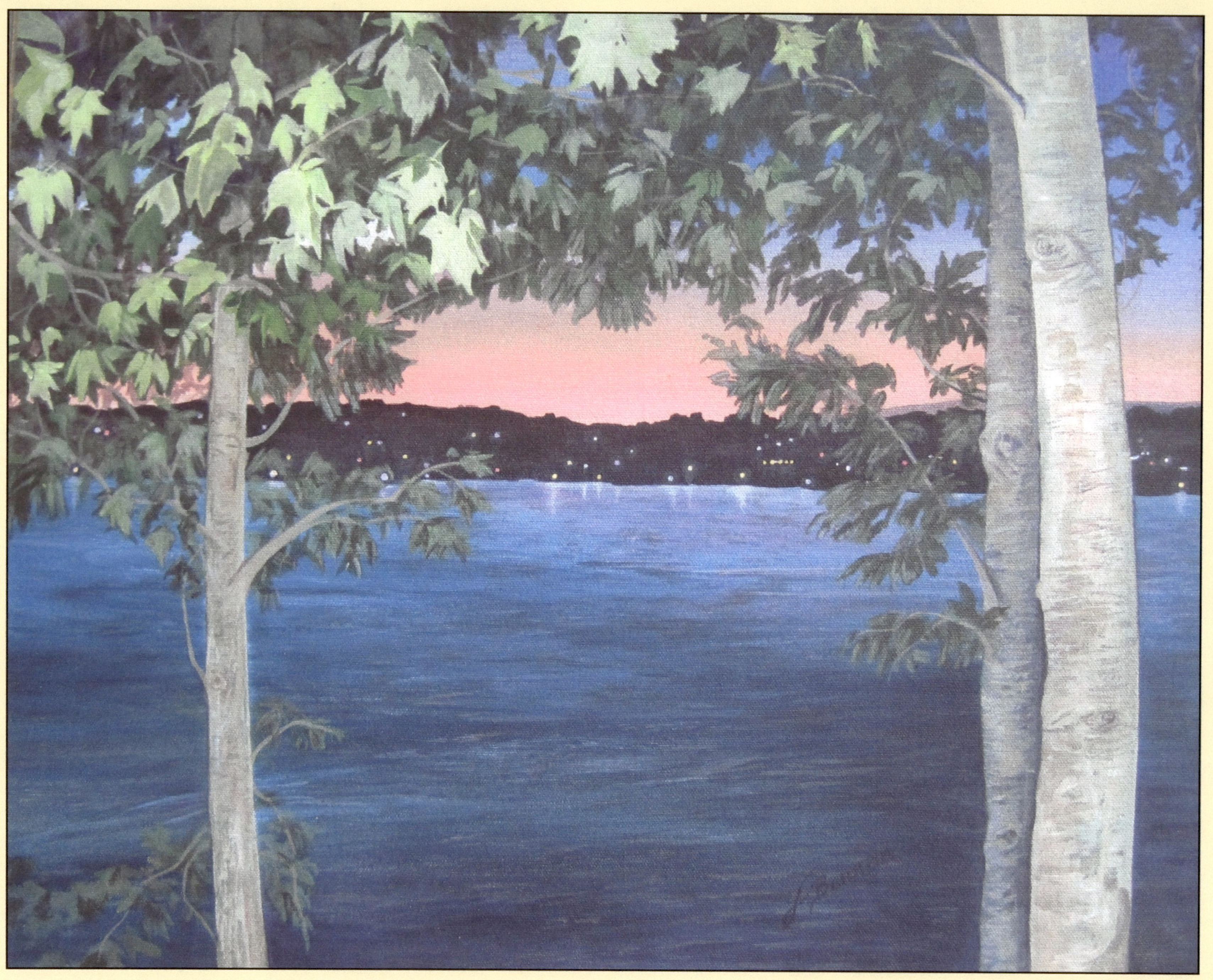

**Night Falls Softly on Jordan Lake II**

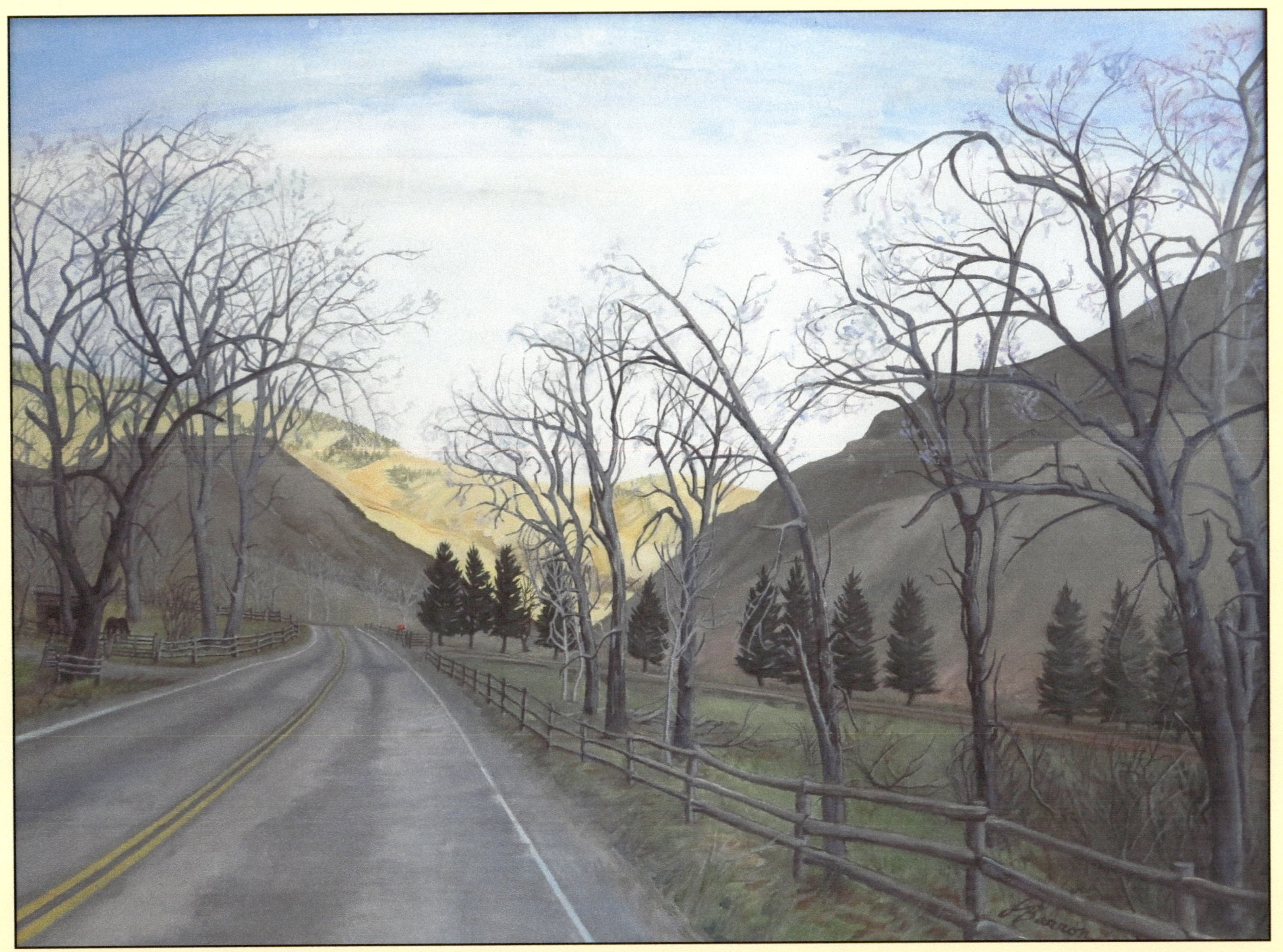



# North Idaho

Fair vistas of north Idaho,
fields of hay and wheat do grow;
mountains blanket endless skies;
American flag so freely flies.
Silver continues to be mined.

Independent folks are kind.
Lumber is a great commodity;
hunting and tourism no oddity.
Wildlife of ascending size;
bed where miles of pine trees rise.

Clear waters snake and shimmer.
This is just a little glimmer.
Thanks to those who leave their
cash.
Take your baggage and your trash.

# II. Faraway Places

## Lucky to Travel

Wherever I've been happy to roam,

I'm most happy to get back home.

It's home that holds the heart.

Leaving plays another part;

awareness ever growing;

foreign lands and people knowing,

history that reaches deep,

memories to always keep.

So different from familiar ground;

a kaleidoscope of sight and sound.

Everywhere you're lucky to travel,

special moments and marvels unravel.

Double lucky to be home...zoomed view from my porch.

My uncle, Douglas Cummings, treated me to a Paris trip in 2000. He shot most of the Paris photos that I painted from. I toured amazing Egypt and Jordan in 2019.  There are no paintings, but I learned camels are cool!

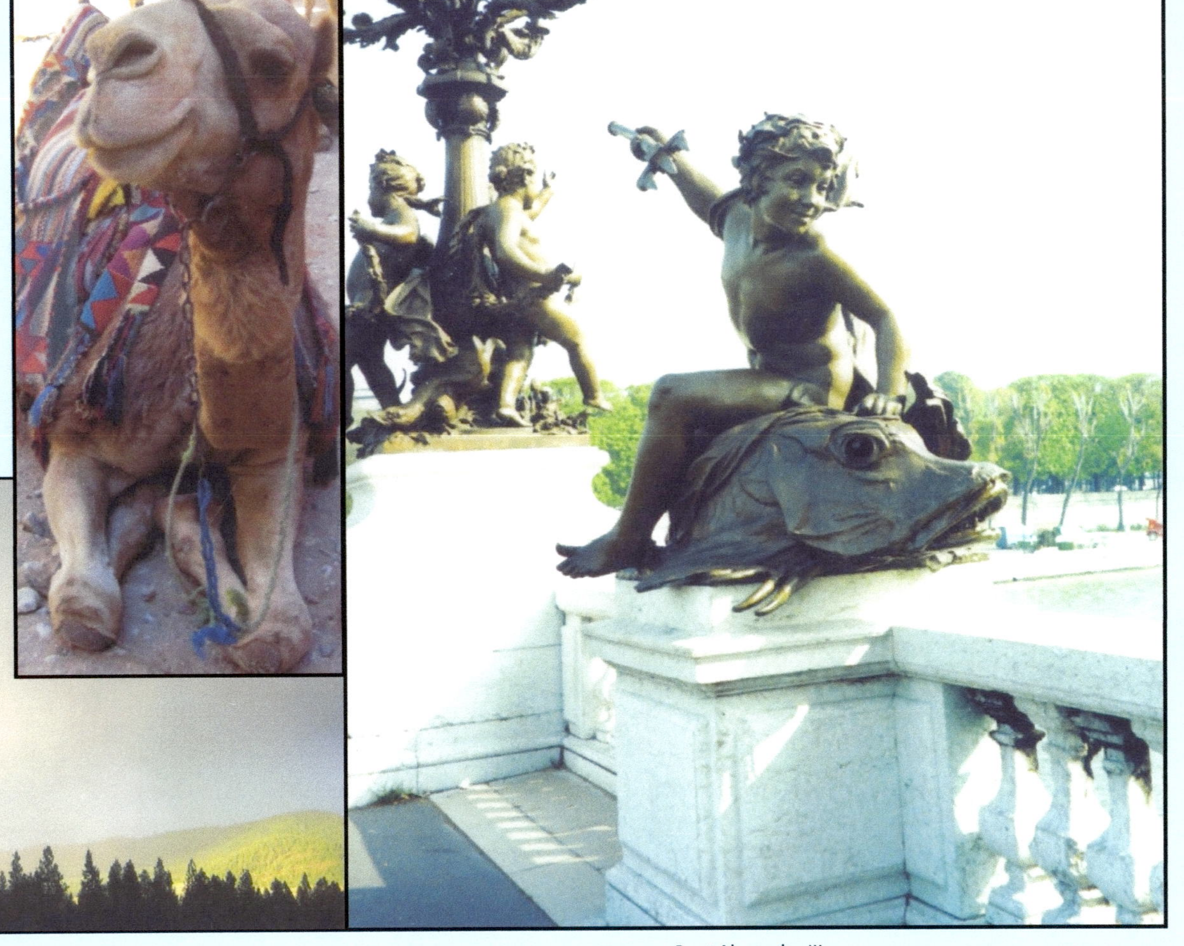

Pont Alexandre III

# Castles

From what I know of castles
most were full of hassles.
Though structurally impressive,
the atmosphere was oppressive.
Dark were the narrow halls.
Tapestries hung on drafty walls.
Light fell in a little puddle,
around a fireplace they'd huddle.
Voices echoed off high stone;
hoofbeats told they weren't alone.
Young warriors would lie dead.
Tired serfs would share their bread.
One didn't eat the first food bite,
and kept an opened eye at night.
Lovely lass would be undone,
fat old man would have his fun.
A festival would be a sight;
a finery, food and fun delight.
If you were a poor visitor,
you might meet the inquisitor.
Better to be a tourist today,
lighter you will get away.

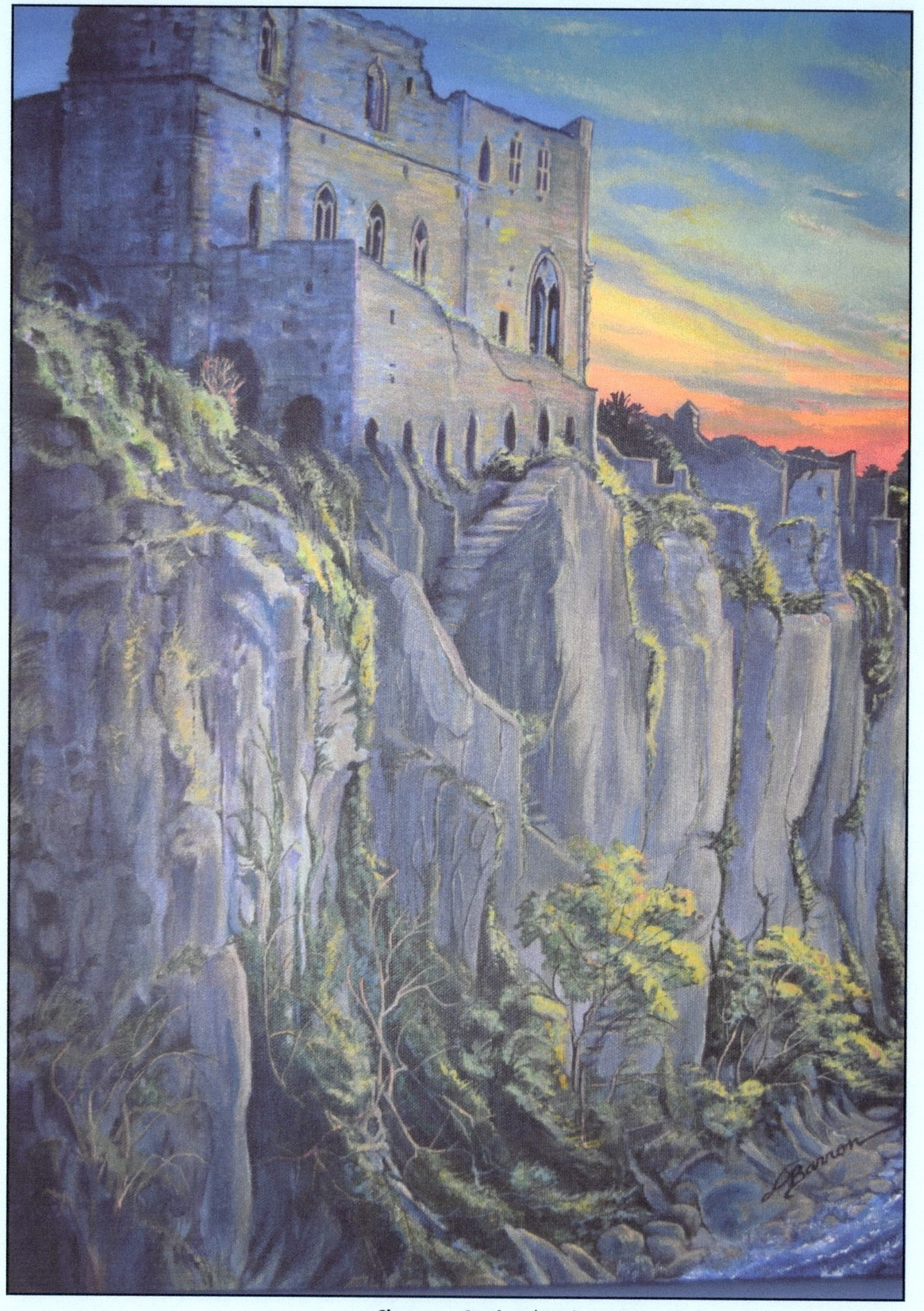

**Chepstow Castle II** | Wales, Painting from photo by Janet Newton

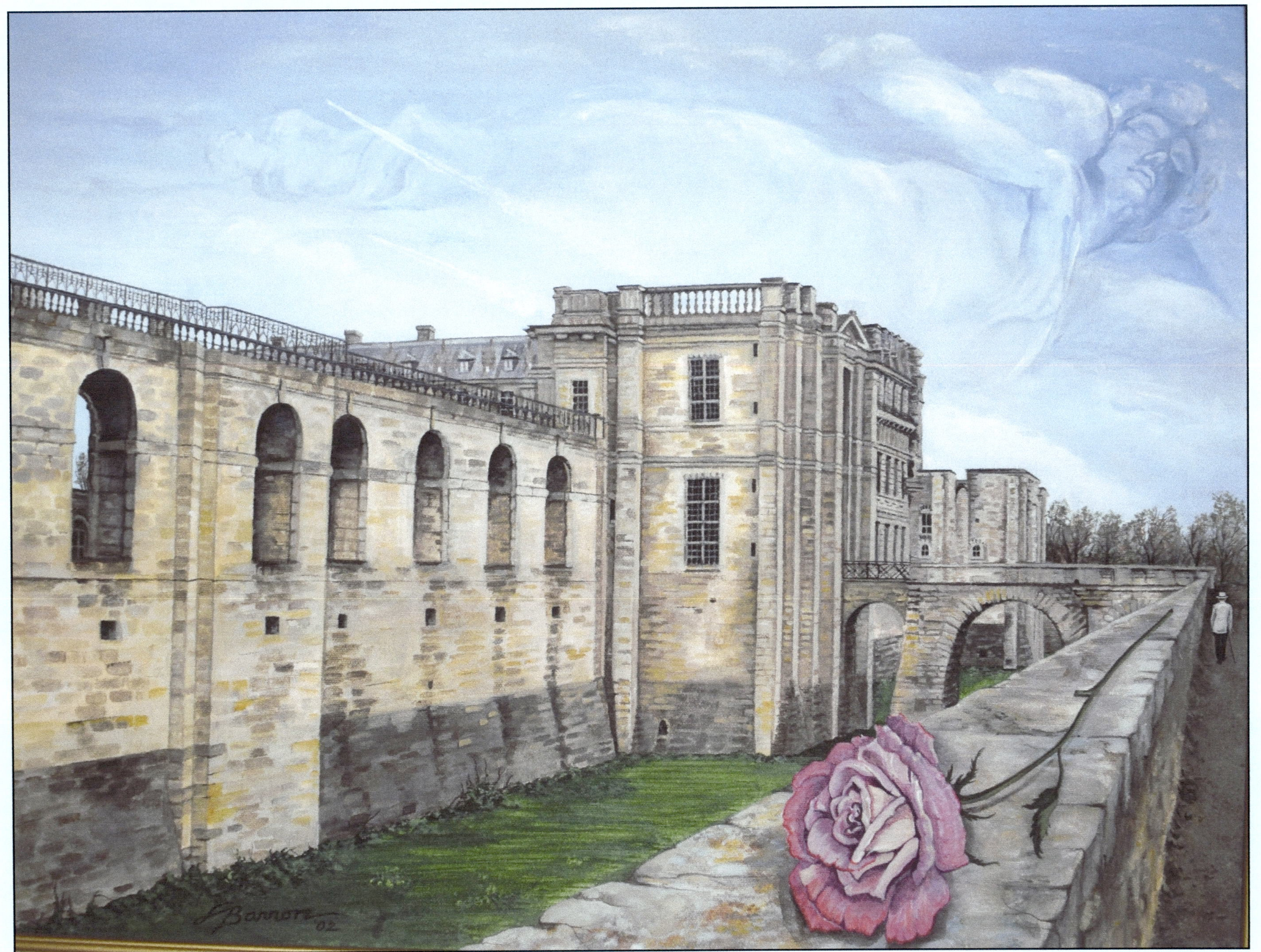

Chateau Vincennes

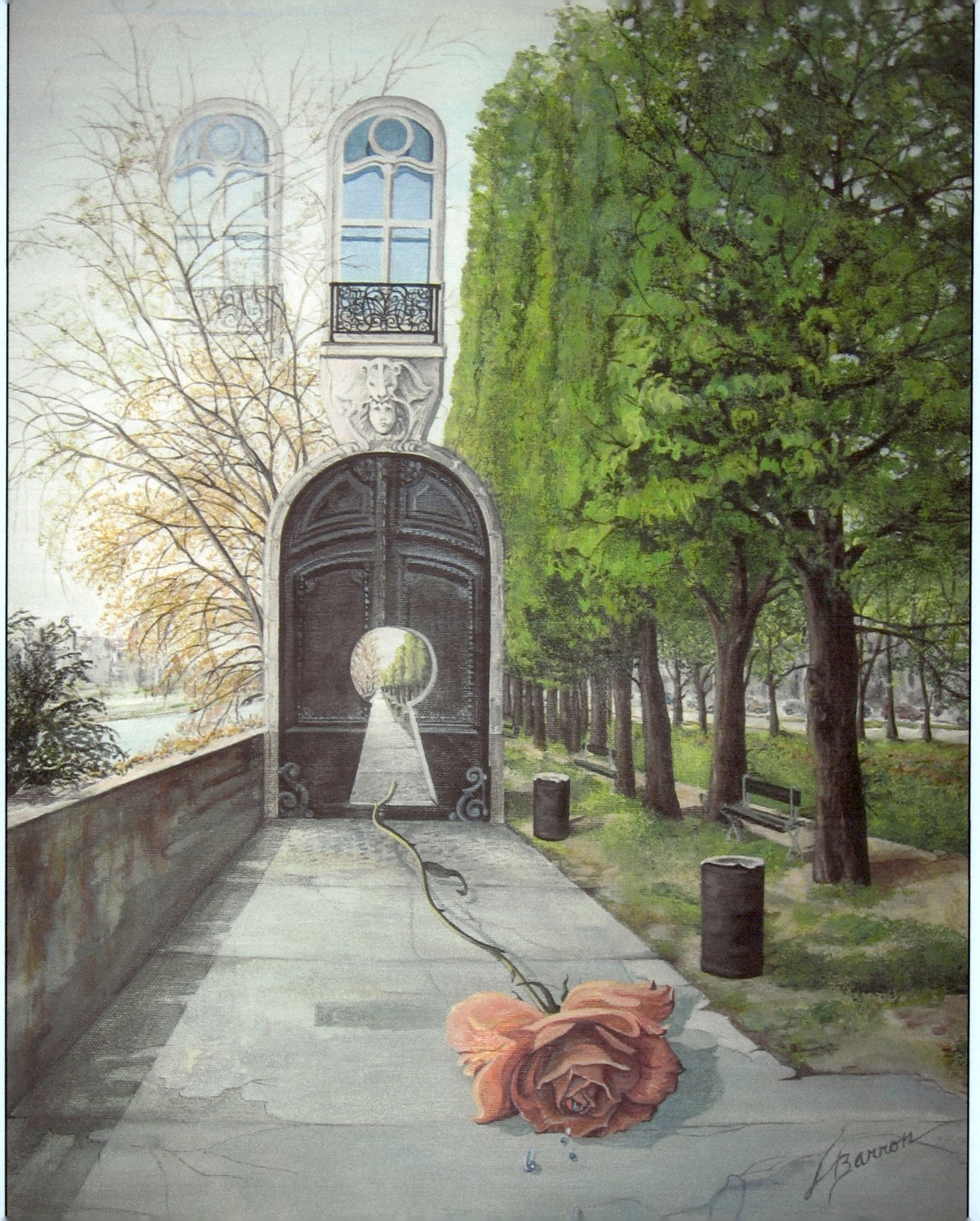

A Rose for Gericault

# A Rose for Gericault

At the Cemetaire Père LaChaise
someone placed a rose with grace,
to honor artist Gericault,
student, relative...who's to know?
A sweet and thoughtful thing to do,
I wished that I could leave one too.
On canvas mine will remain fresh,
with beloved city to mesh.
A riding accident left him ill;
thirty-three years were all he'd fill.
A blossom pinched in 1824;
artwork that opened many a door.
He's been gone these countless years.
Still, the rose must shed some tears.

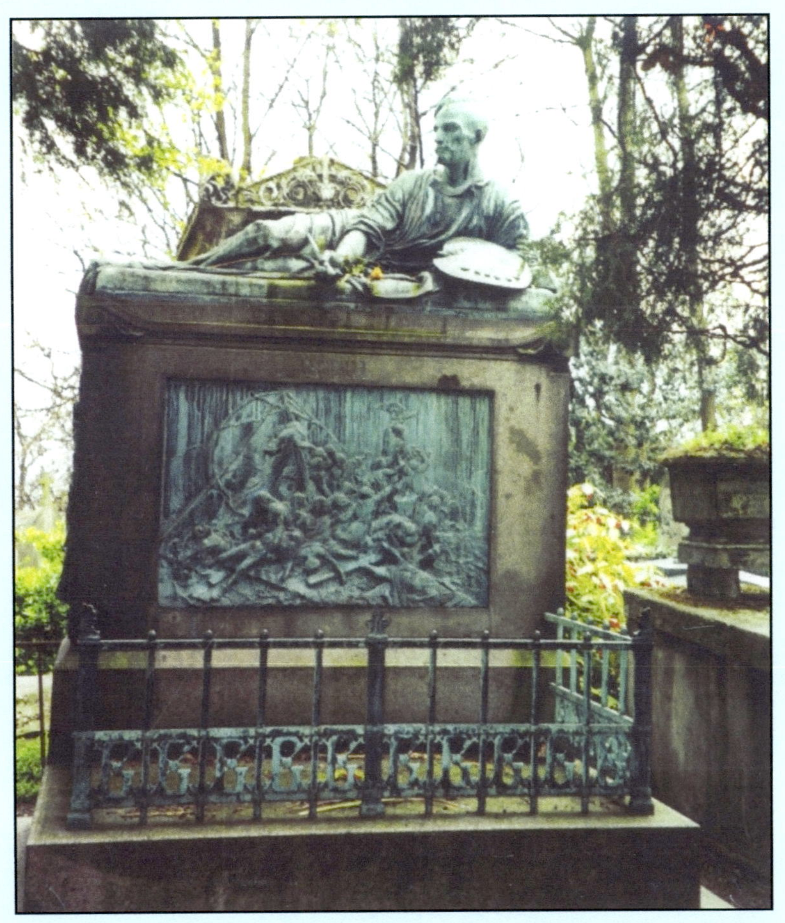

On the tomb of Theodore Gericault, Père LaChaise
Cemetaire, the yellow rose is visible.

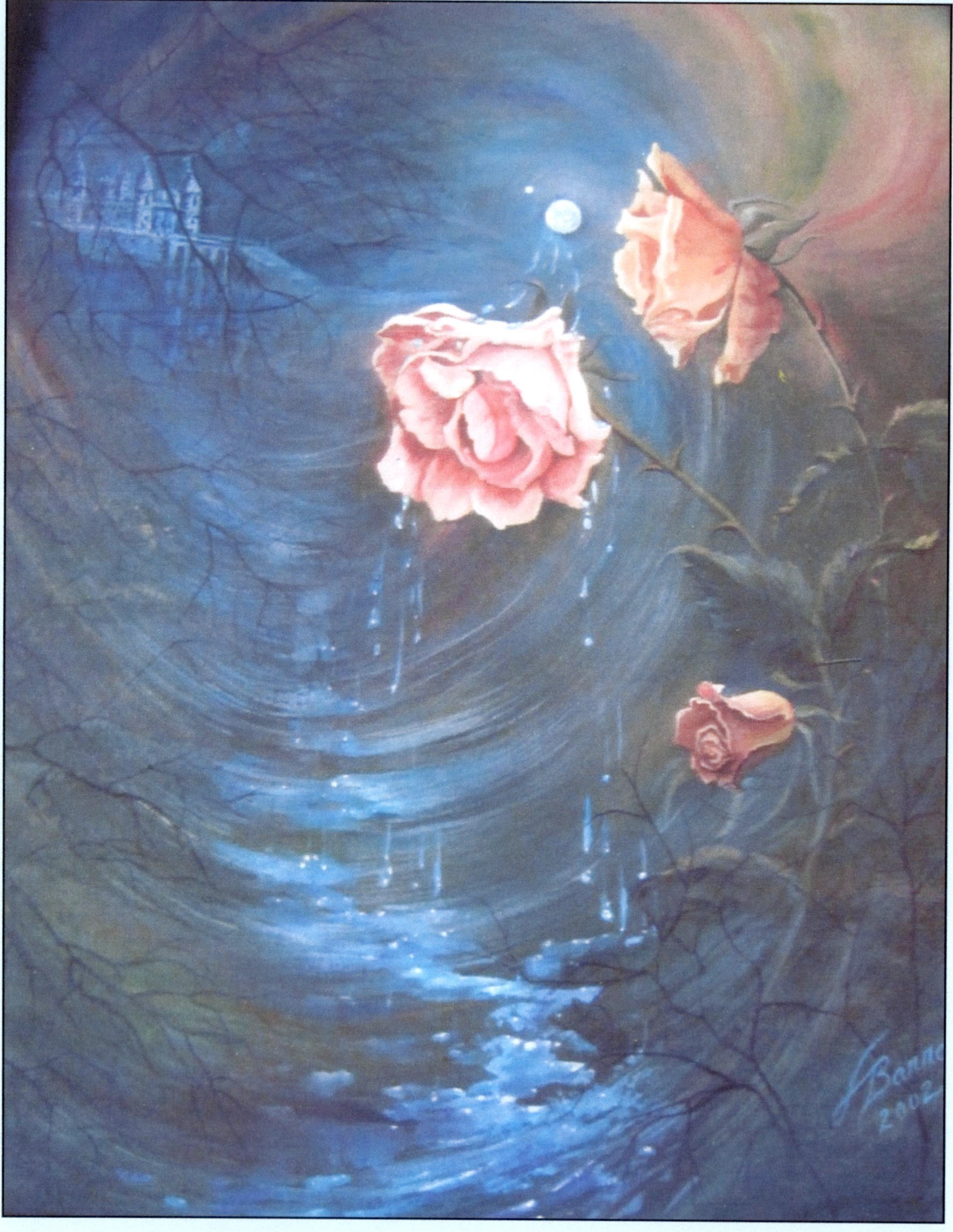

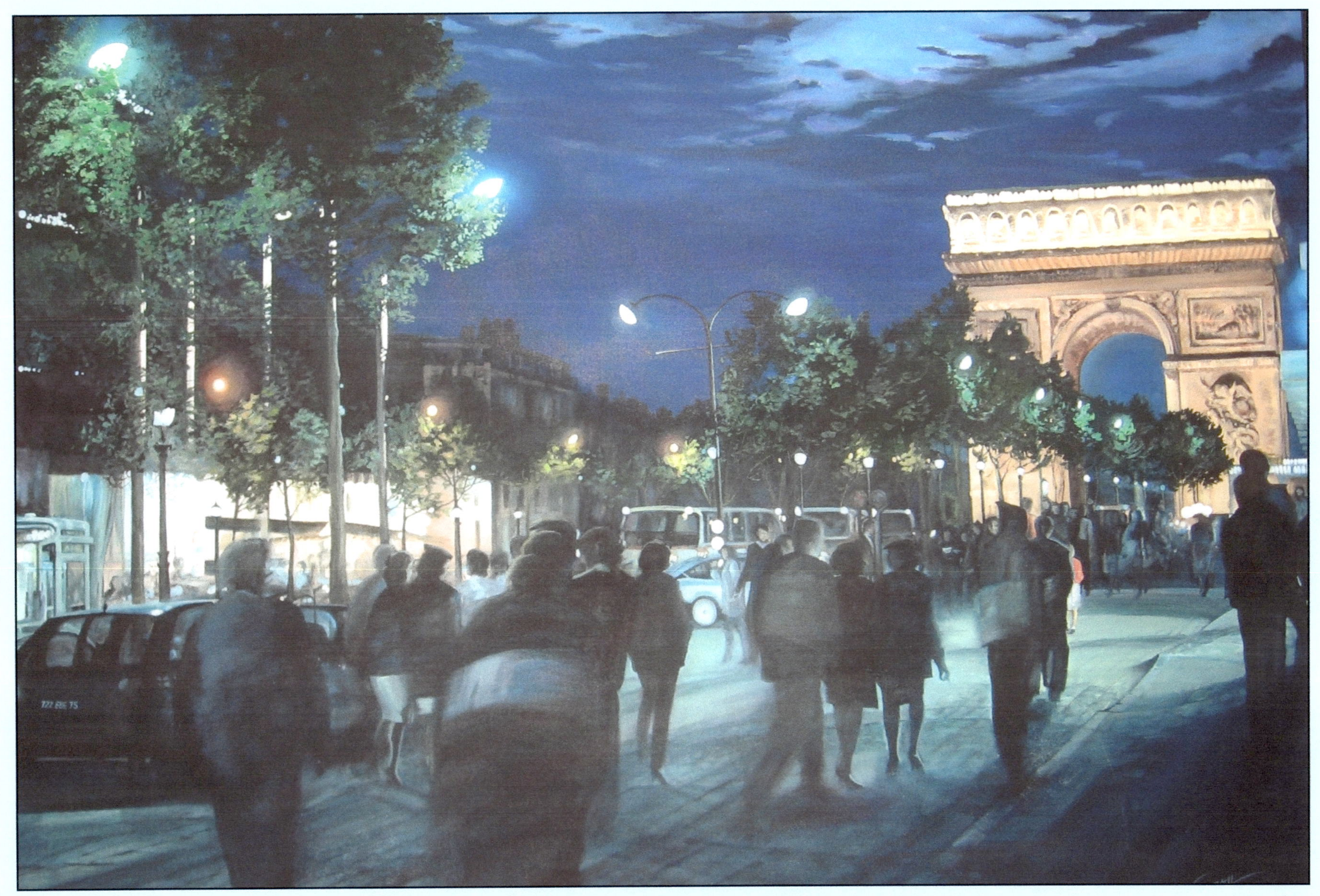

Avec

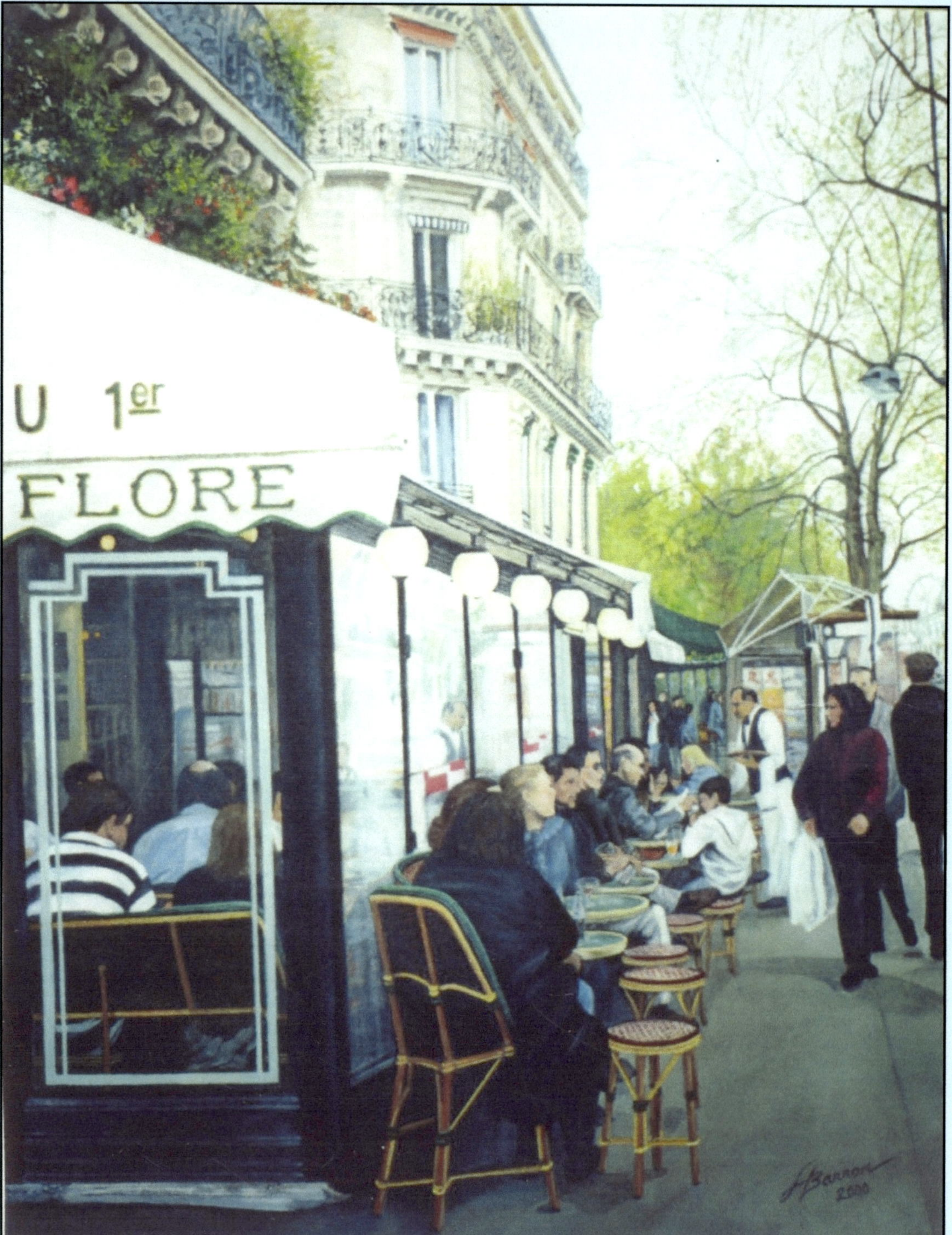


Café de Flore

# The Postcard
## J. L. Barrault

Raised above the River Seine,
sidewalks seem to never end.
Notre Dame looms...other side,
tour boat guest will get a ride.
Booths with paper wares for sale,
backed against the upper rail,
try to catch the tourist's eye,
most are simply strolling by.
Shadows pattern the concrete,
dancing brightly at their feet.
Caught by postcards on a rack;
one I would be taking back.
 A vintage image in black and white;
an actor in costume...that's right.
Once home I search this man,
watch the film...learn what I can.
In this 1945 classic French feature,
he plays a sad, downtrodden creature.
By day he must pretend and smile;
his heart is broken all the while.
His love was not to be returned.
His hopes and dreams were spurned.
This face, intense and gaunt,
entrenched...my mind to haunt.
I paint him in monochromatic blue.
His photo...justice I cannot do.

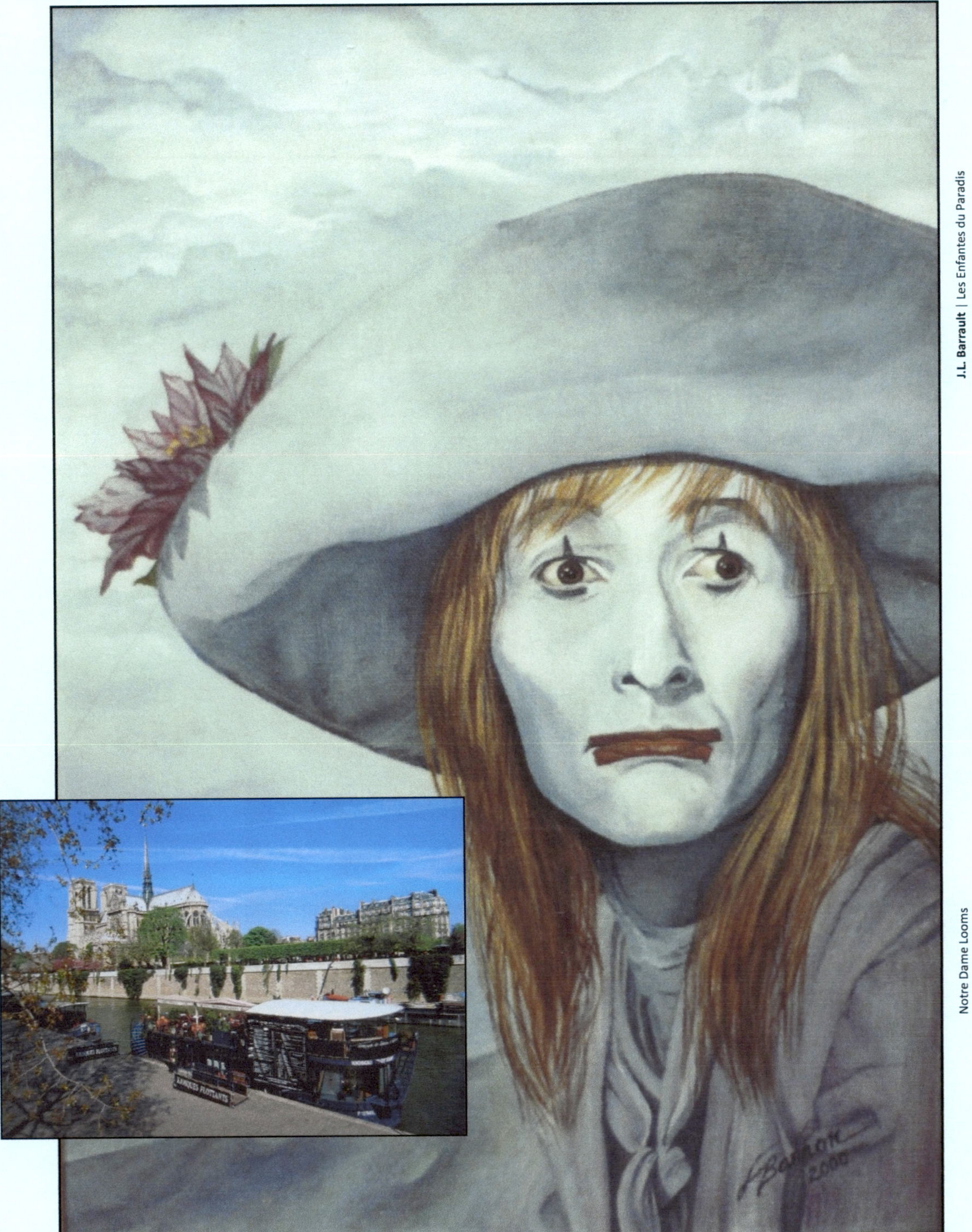



23

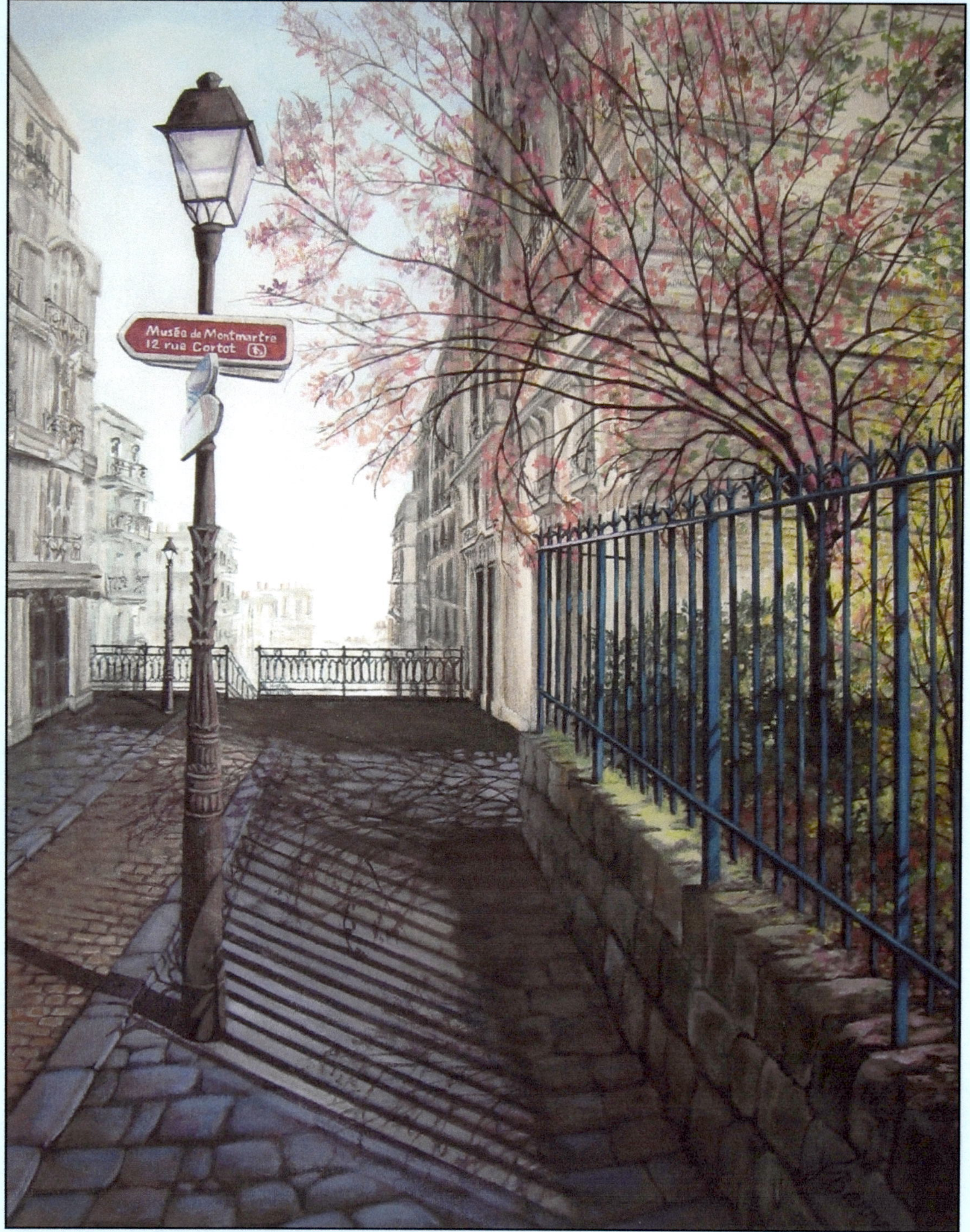

Musée de Montmartre
12 rue Cortot



Le Passant

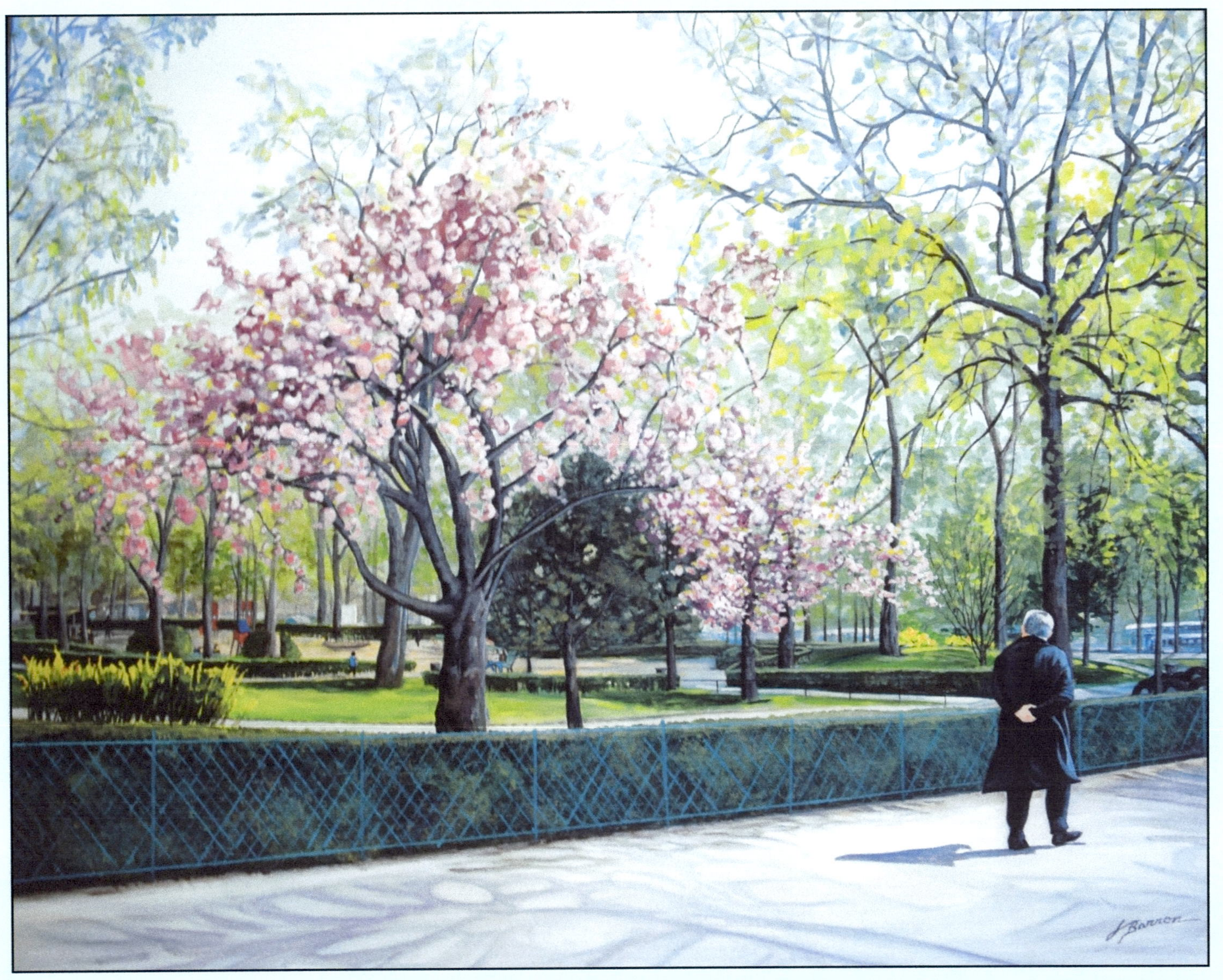

Saunter Near the Park

# Saunter Near the Park

He walks this route most every day;
no need to think about the way.
He smiles at children as they play.
Flowers gift him colors gay.

He feels good fortune as he goes;
listens to the choir of crows;
works hard...his portfolio grows;
of gratitude are the seeds he sows.

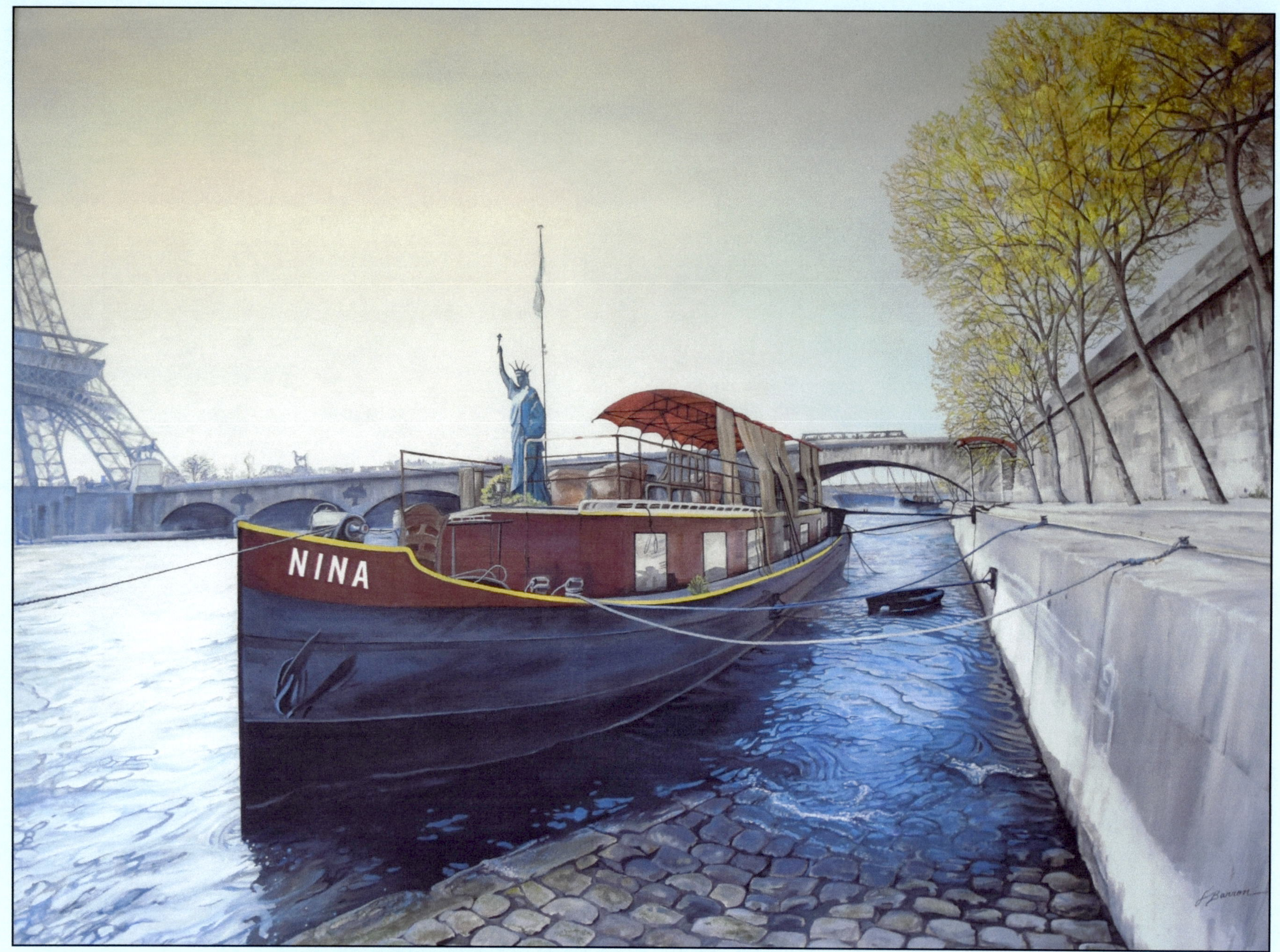

Nina

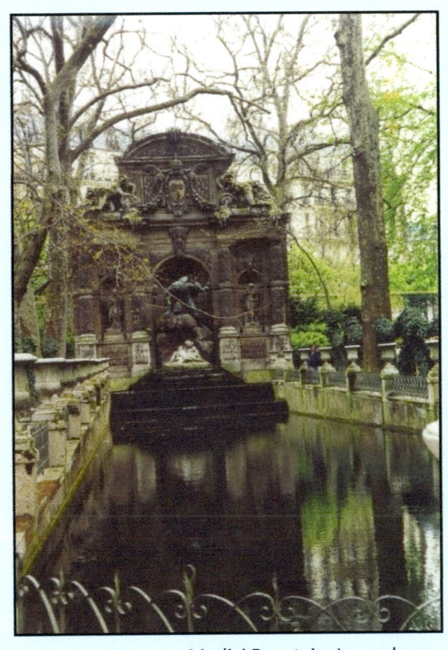

Medici Fountain, Luxembourg

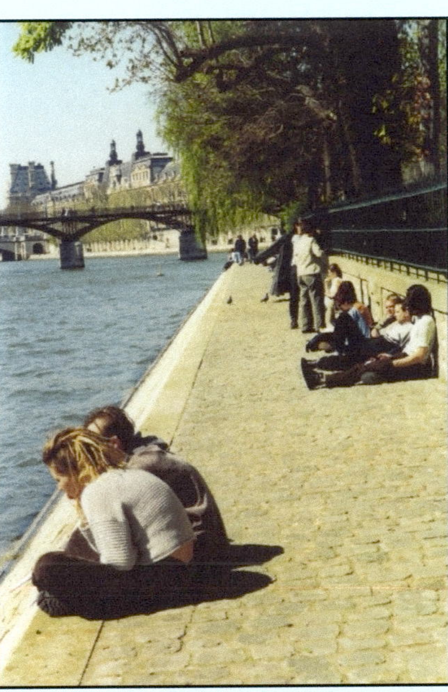

Below the garden on The Point

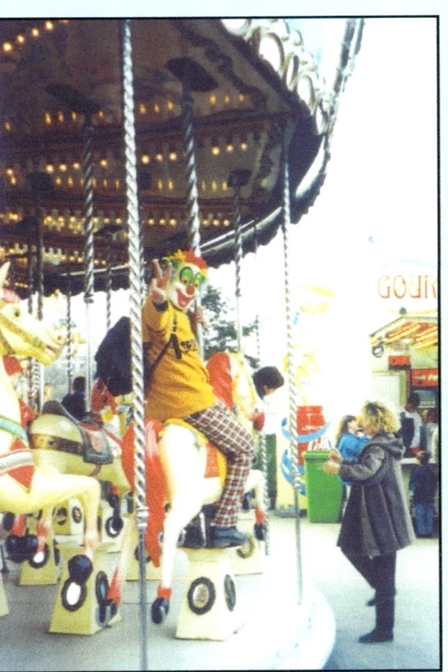

Carousel by the Eiffel Tower

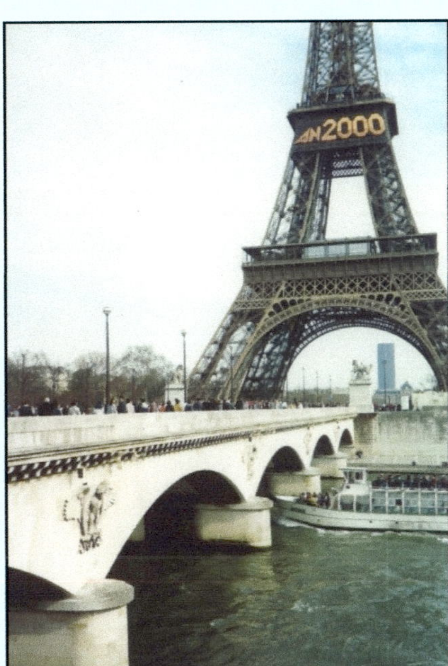

2000 lit

# Paris

Paris…what a wondrous place to be,

beauty all around to see.

Pont Alexandre III decorated to the hilt,

fanciful statues some with gilt.

Fit for kings and queens to tread,

near to where their lives were bled.

The Eiffel Tower with 2000 lit,

a walk to the point to garden sit.

Careful…in the Seine you'll fall,

where lovers sit against the wall.

Notre Dame, Basilique du Sacre Coeur,

Arc de Triomphe and the Louvre lure.

Montmartre's hilly cobbled lanes,

humongous doors…stacked window panes.

The Medici fountain's stunning calm,

covered in mossy timeless balm.

There's really all too much to share.

Maybe someday you'll go there.

Seat-belted for the return flight stint,

I've 300 photos yet to print.

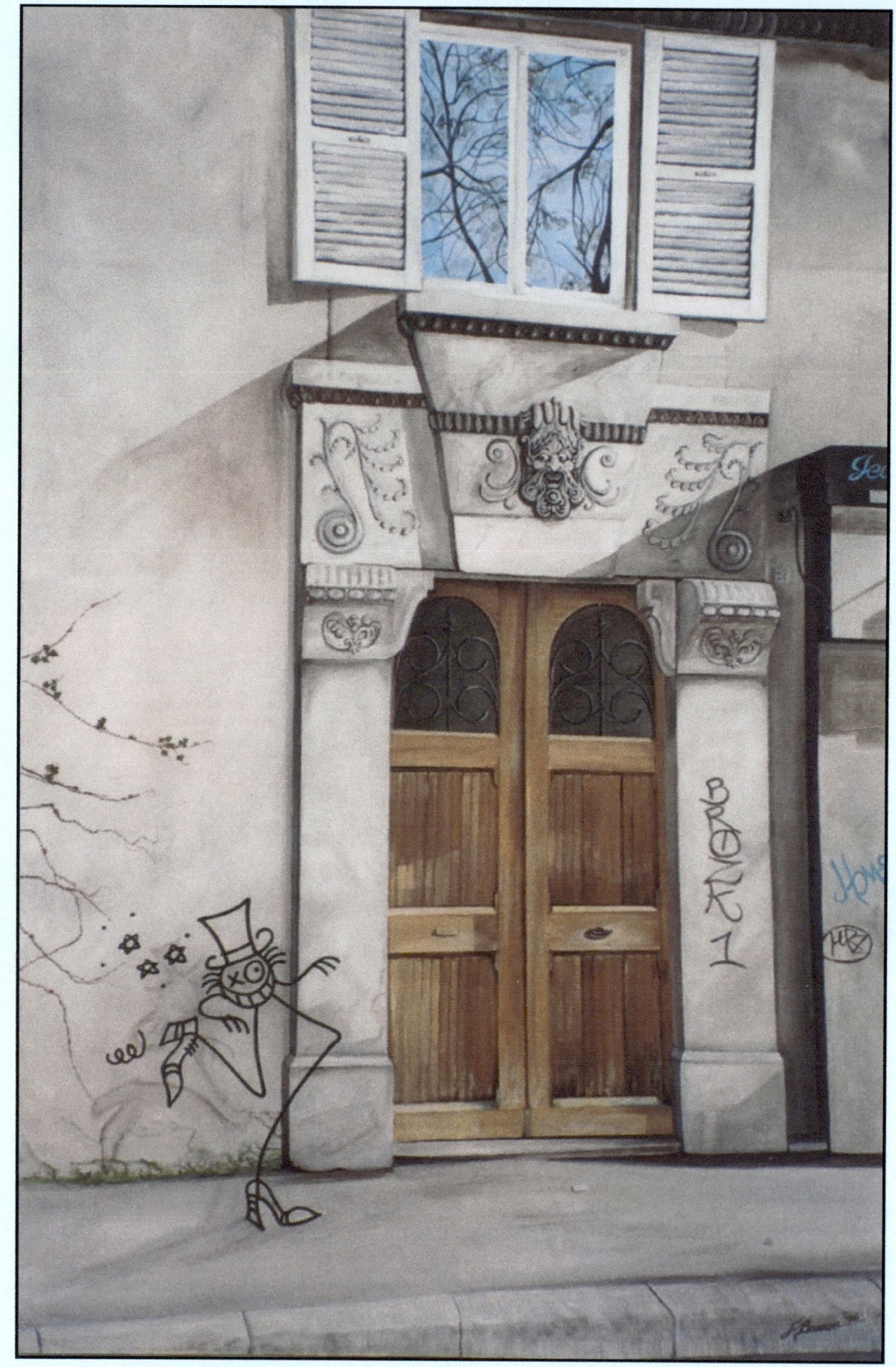

# Graffiti on the Move

An artist's hand does undertake;

delight or detriment...like or berate.

Lines upon the surface flat

show skill or colors in a splat.

A message it may clearly state;

the wall disfigured...nerves do grate.

Imagine that this figure's alive,

flowing with personality and drive.

Would he deserve our sympathy,

appreciation or empathy?


**YOU** might be simply grossly garish

or quite famous like this one in Paris.

You're just stuck there day after day.

**If only you could walk away.**

Different people would see your grandeur

and view you with enlightened candor.

If on a boxcar you'll go far.

Why not grace the neighborhood bar?

If on a mural you'd be plural.

On a barn you'd enjoy being rural.

If you could strut across the street

just think of all the kids you'd greet.

In making them smile you'd stay for awhile

upon the wall of grey concrete,

frozen but feeling more complete.

If only you could go wherever,

life would be a great endeavor.

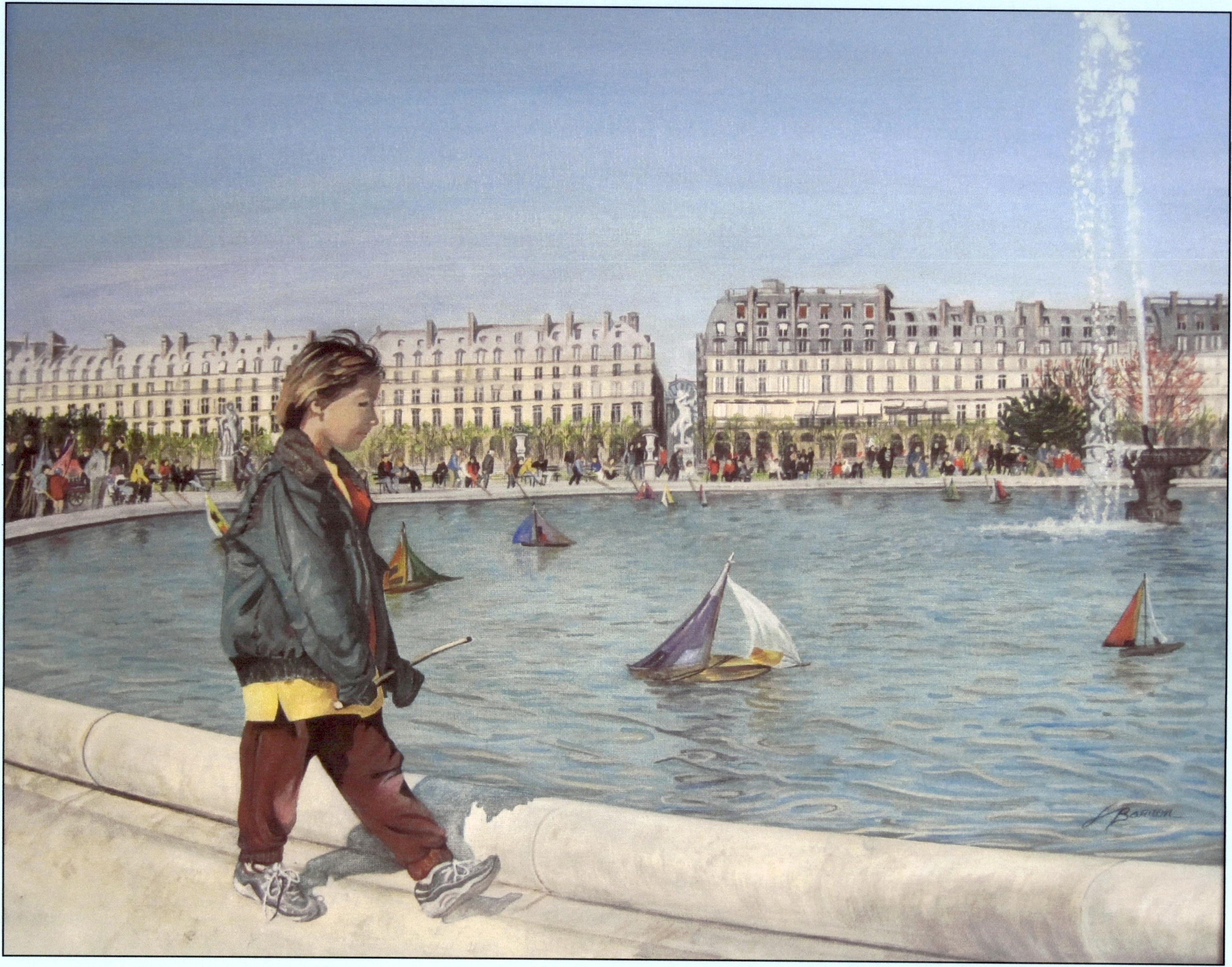

**Sail Away**

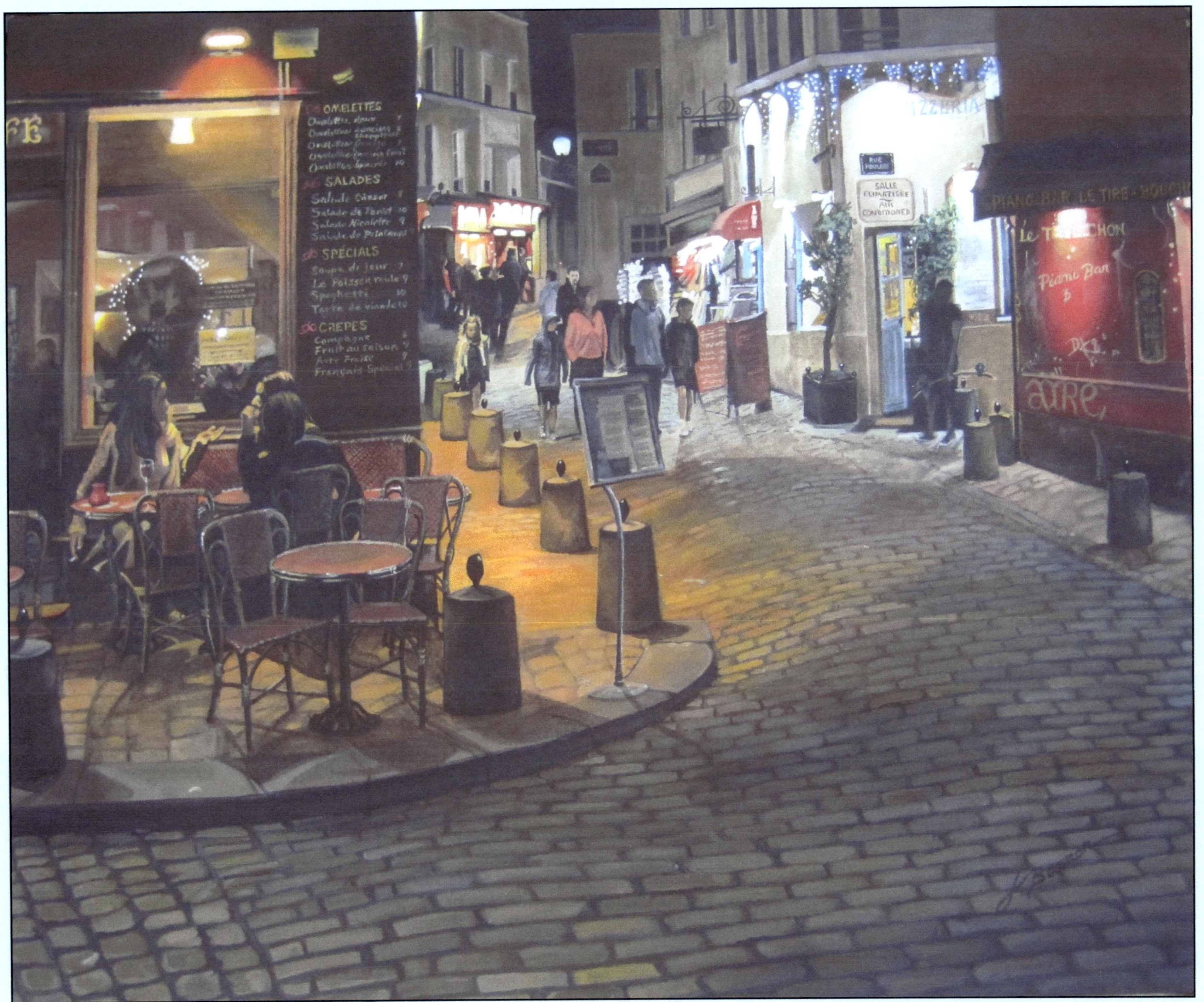

**Evening in Paris** | This and the following two paintings were from photographs and commissions by a patron, Lee.

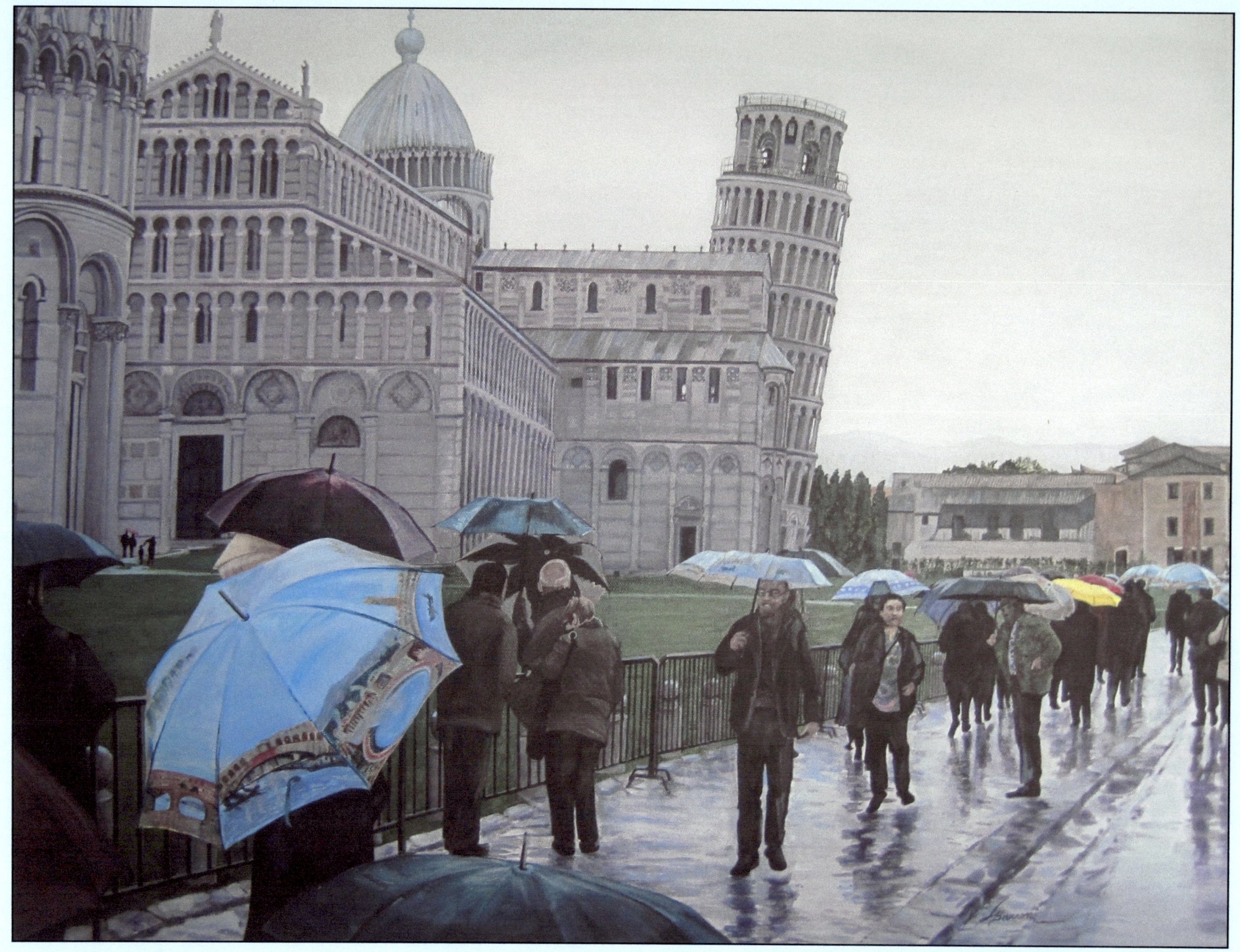

**Rainy Day in Pisa**

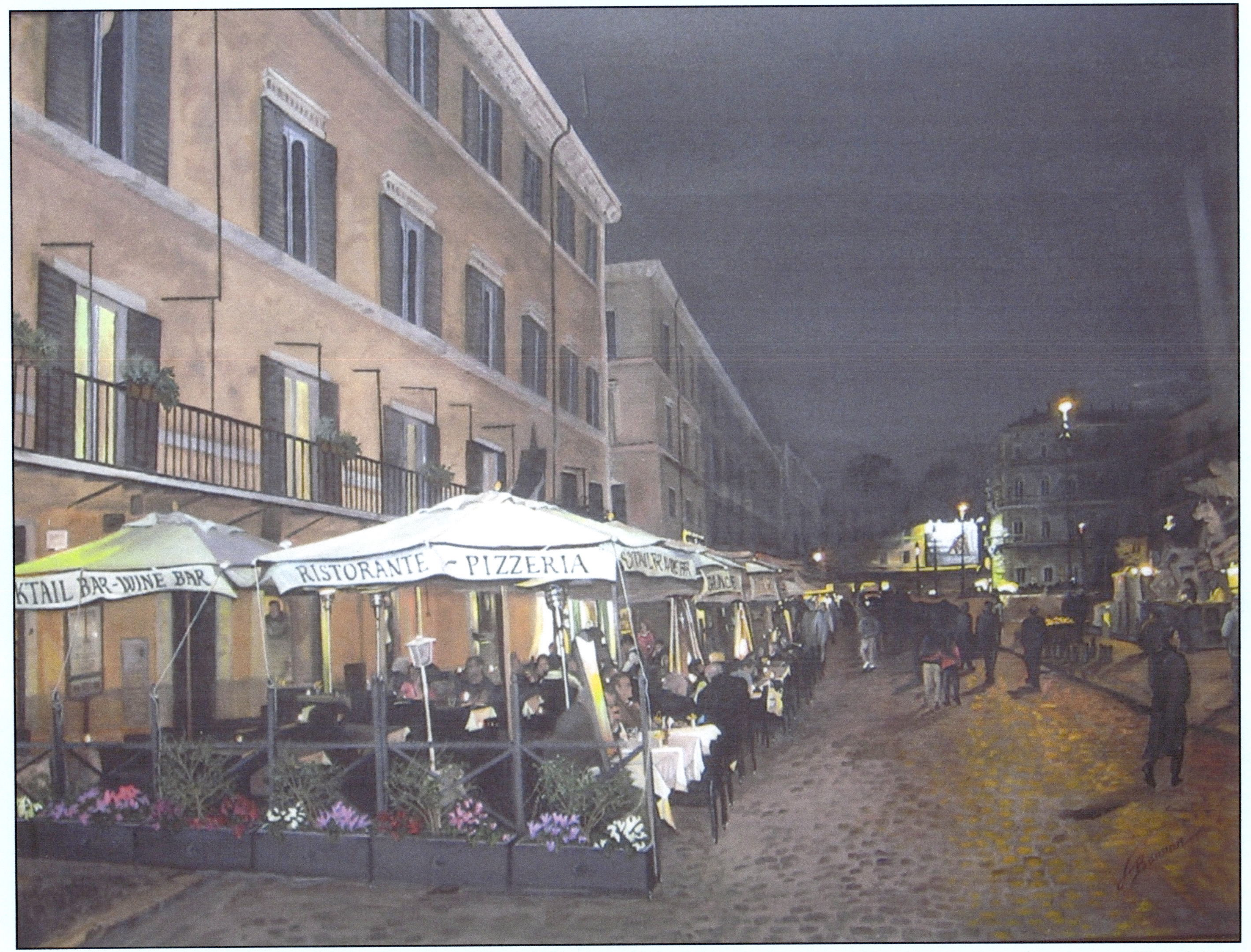


Promande in Italy

# III. More Whimsical

## Dreamscapes

Conscious brain has been detained;

Illogical thoughts have come unchained.

Vivid colors aren't denied,

story lines not unified.

Few are traced from waking day,

most unwind in random way.

A relief from which to wake?

Events you'd rather not partake?

*Some are frightful, others delightful,*

*some are amusing, others confusing,*

*some are alarming, others charming.*

Even though I'm old and gray,

often years have flown away.

Re-enactments of desire,

I romp in mindless misty mire.

Many are just plain weird,

indicative of how my mind is geared?

Surrealists have been called deranged,

things we know are re-arranged.

If I could paint it all just right,

I'd show you what I see at night.

Then I think, "Why would you care?"

Only I was taken there.

Say, "I just had the strangest dream."

No...they're not even on your team.

That's a switch off of their hearing.

Only their dreams are endearing.

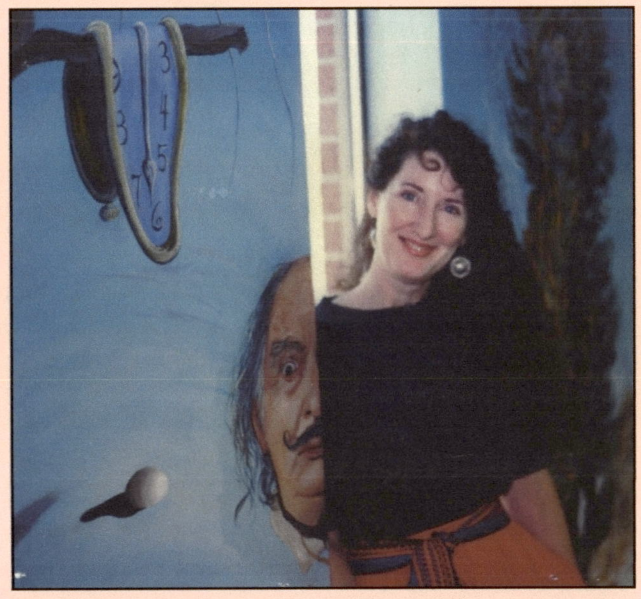

The high school class-room walls were surrounded by my painted murals. Here I smile in 1995 (age 47).

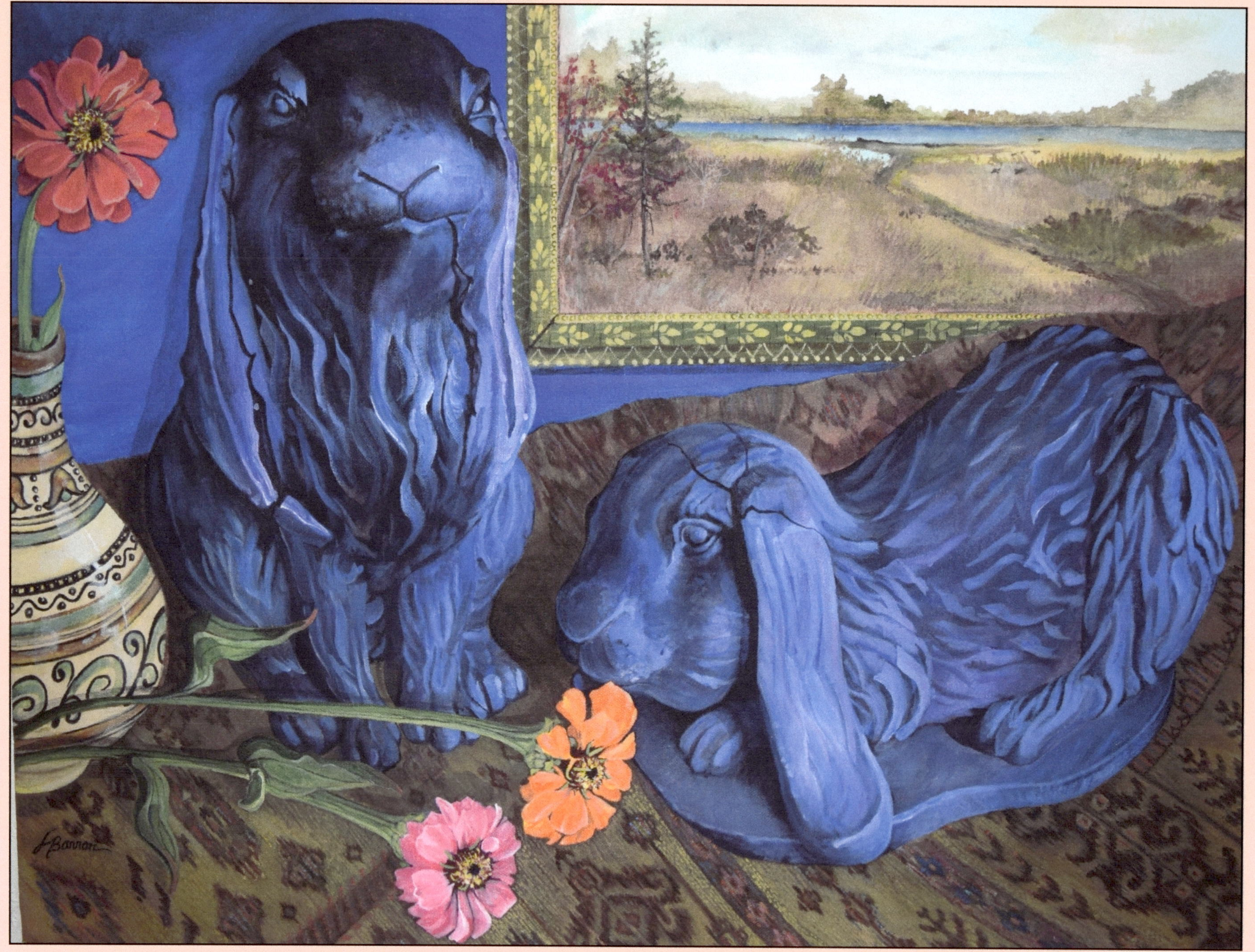

**Color Trip**

# Color Trip

There's a color that's of green/gold/brown,
sometimes in dried nature found.
I guess it's greeny browny gold,
one that seems so very old.
Millennium of trod on earth,
roiled river twice its girth,
jars of childhood pennies tarnished,
foreign foods with spices garnished,
plentiful at farms and zoos,
minus green in favored booze,
carpets in Victorian rooms,
faded murals in ancient tombs,
gleaming eyes of some I know,
leaves beneath the melting snow.
It's soft and quiet all around,
no brazen primary to be found.
If a few happen to abound,
it tempers them into the ground.
It soothes and gives one pleasure...
ovation for this well-done treasure.

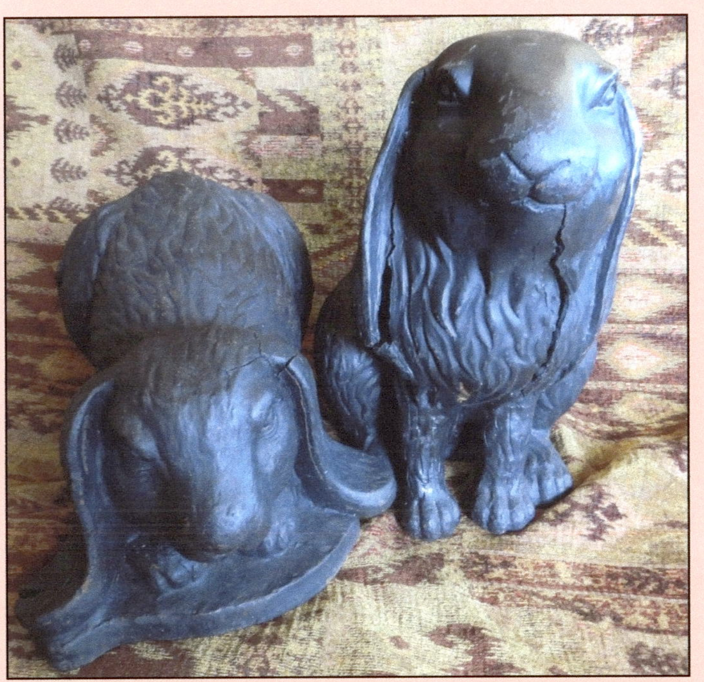

Inspiration photo,
antique 16" cast-iron hares

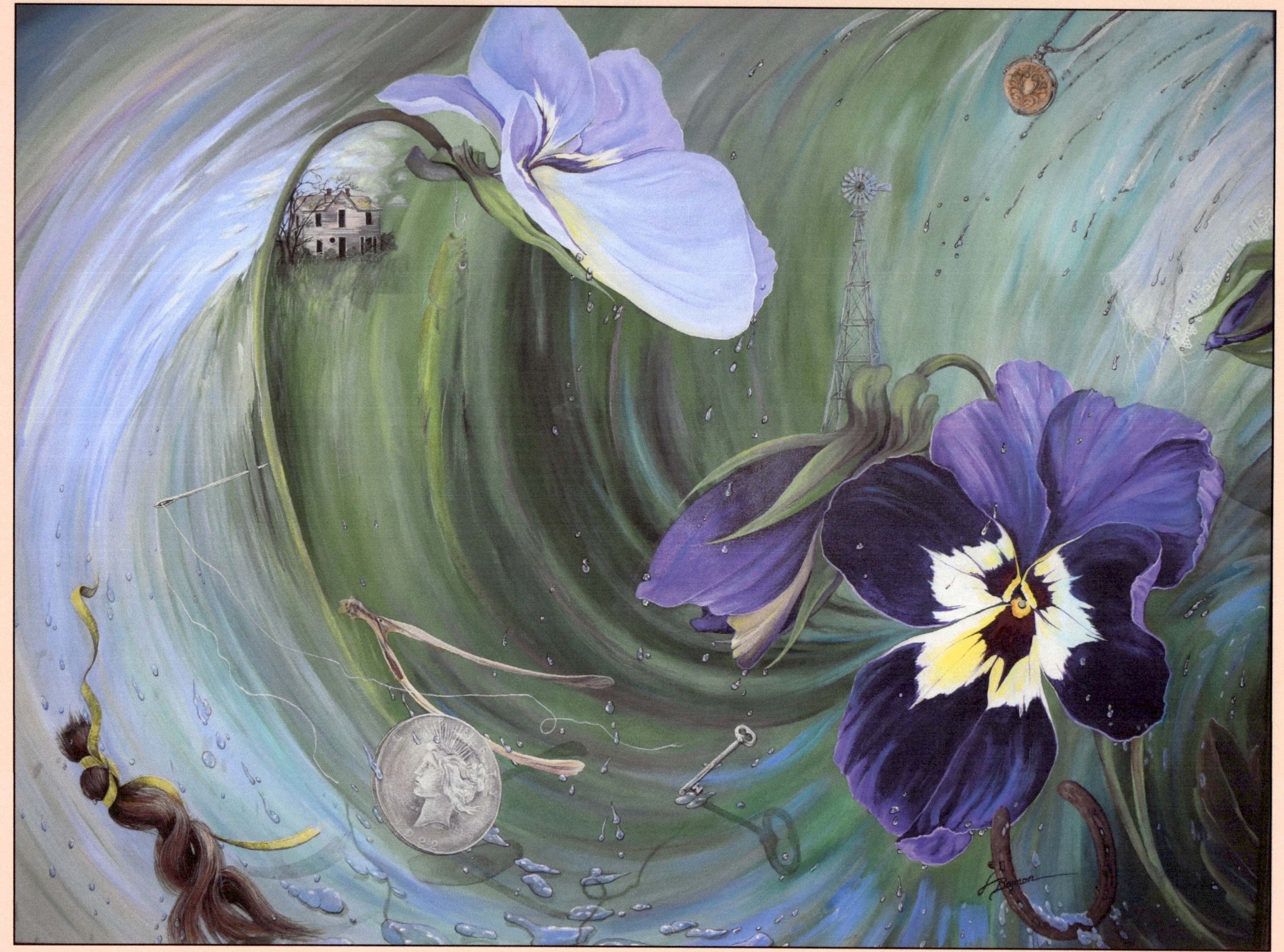

**Stitch in Time**

# Stitch in Time

I can never get enough

of rituals and antique stuff.

Lace curtains blowing in the breeze,

tarnished coins and skeleton keys,

horse shoe up to catch good luck,

fish caught standing in the muck,

heirloom cactus with which I'm stuck,

home-made quilt around to tuck.

A locket speaks sad family tale,

mother to sons as they stand at the rail,

farewell...as they'll sail the sea,

one to each..."*Remember me.*"

A sense of purpose and of place,

washed away in a time erase.

It wasn't always good, you see.

It's tomorrow where you're meant to be.

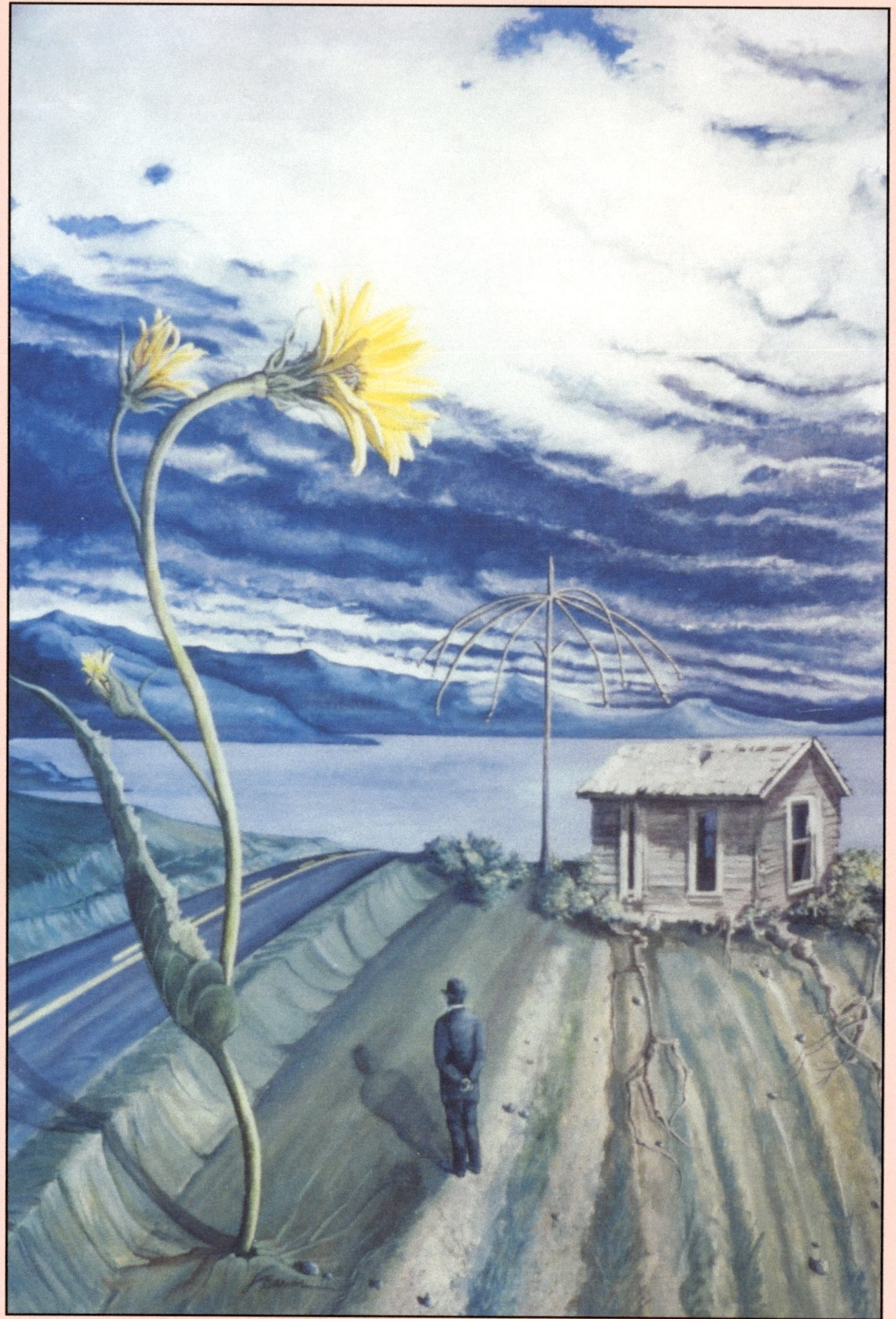

Reminisce

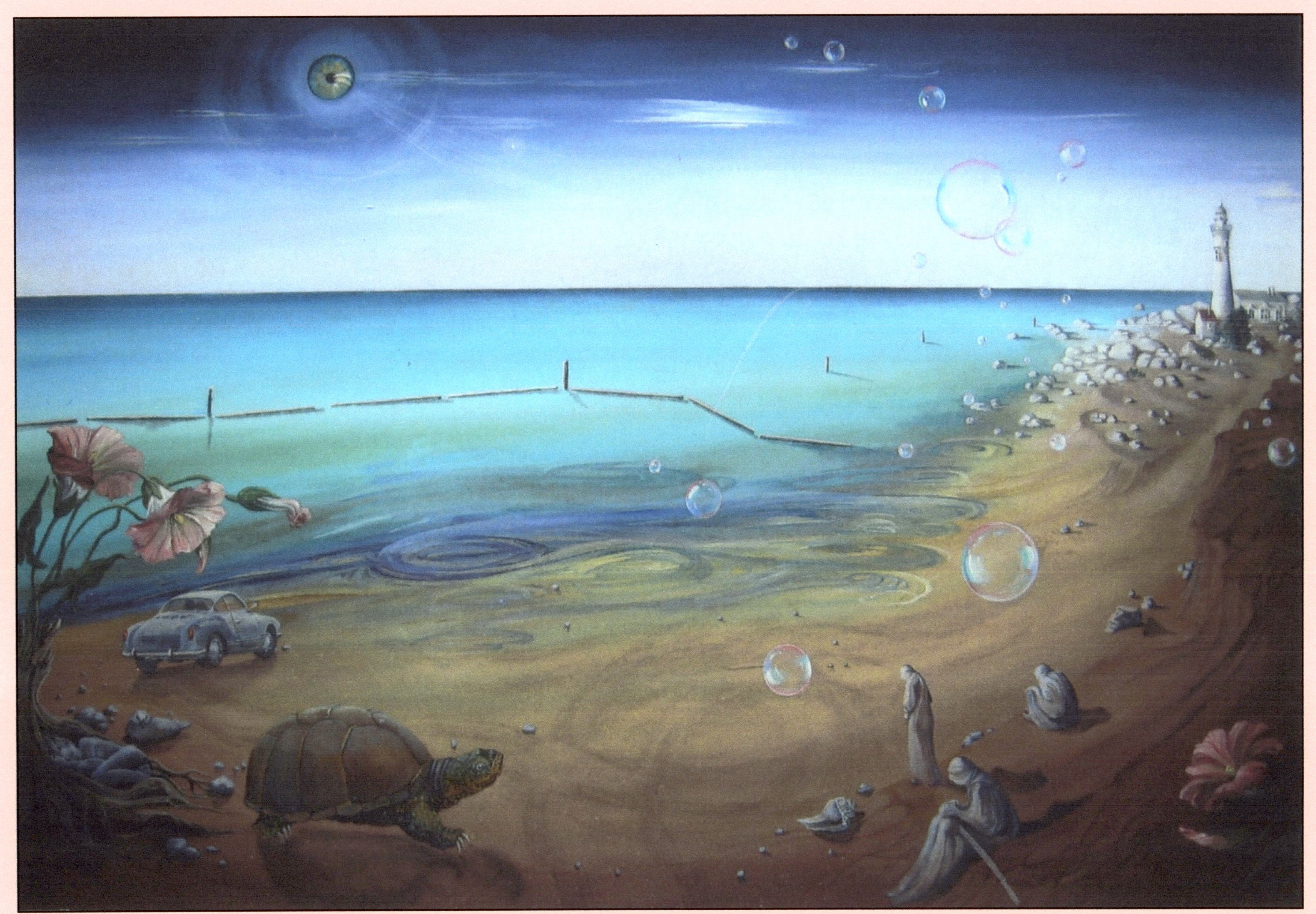

**Date Drive**

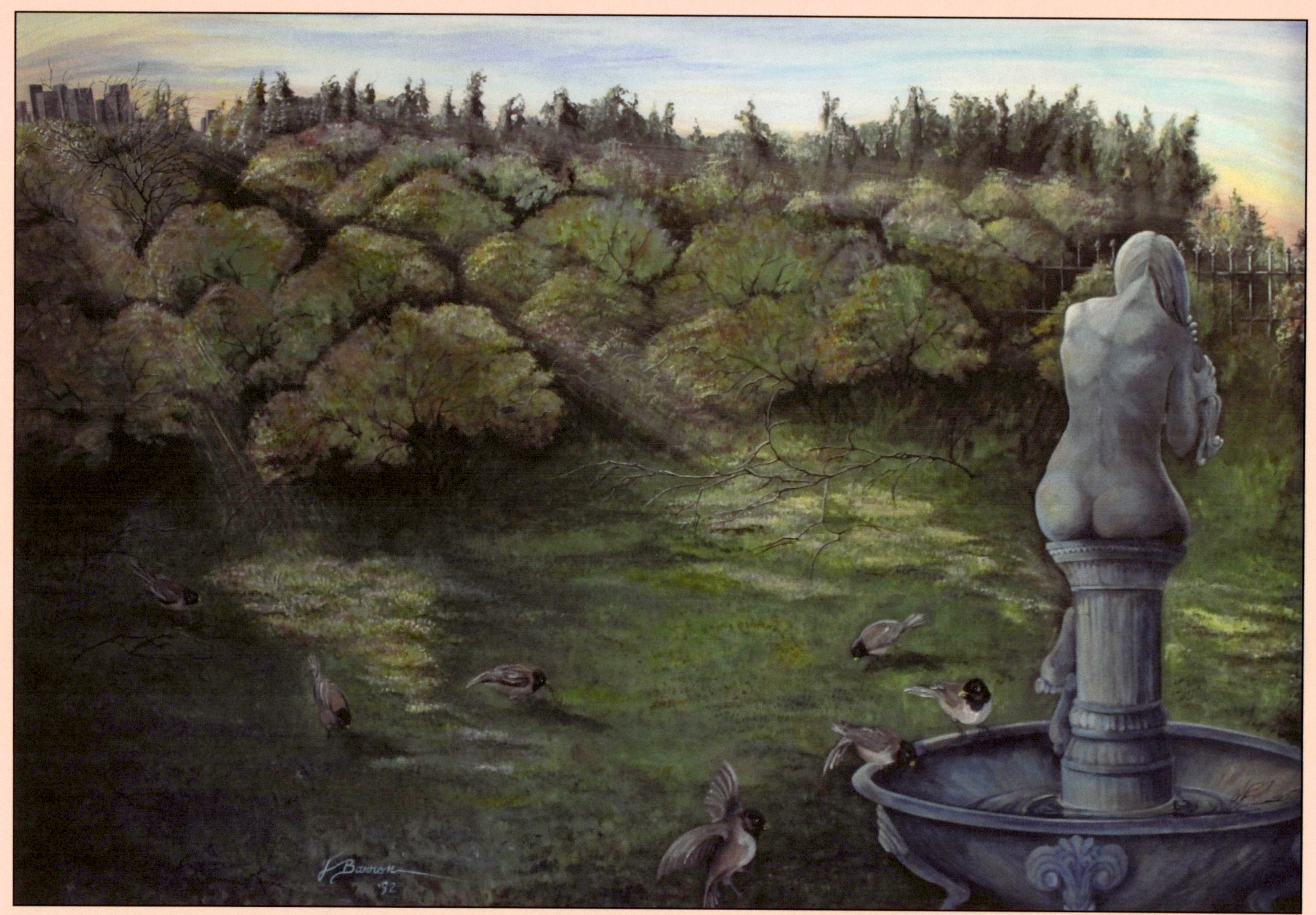

**Encroachment**

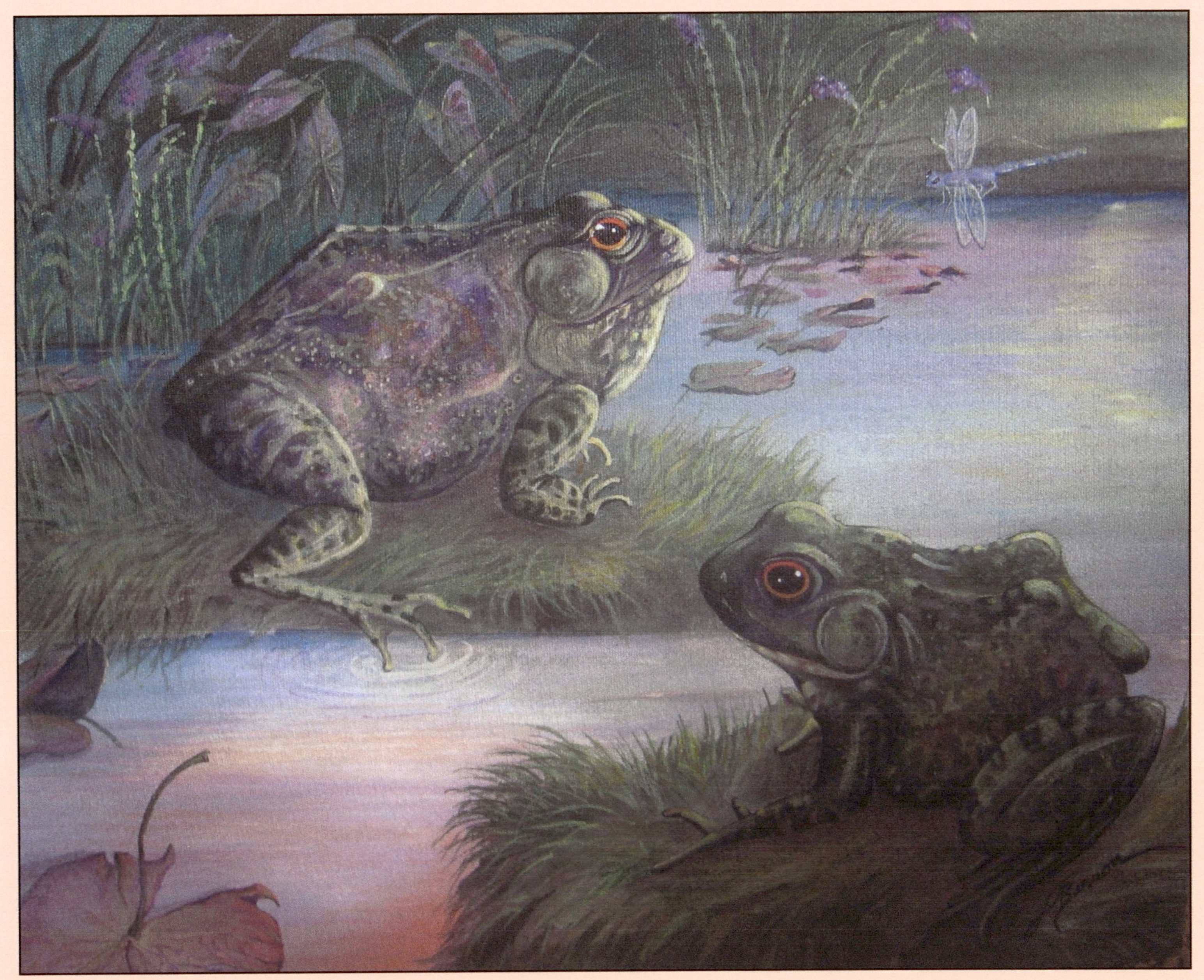

Morning Friends

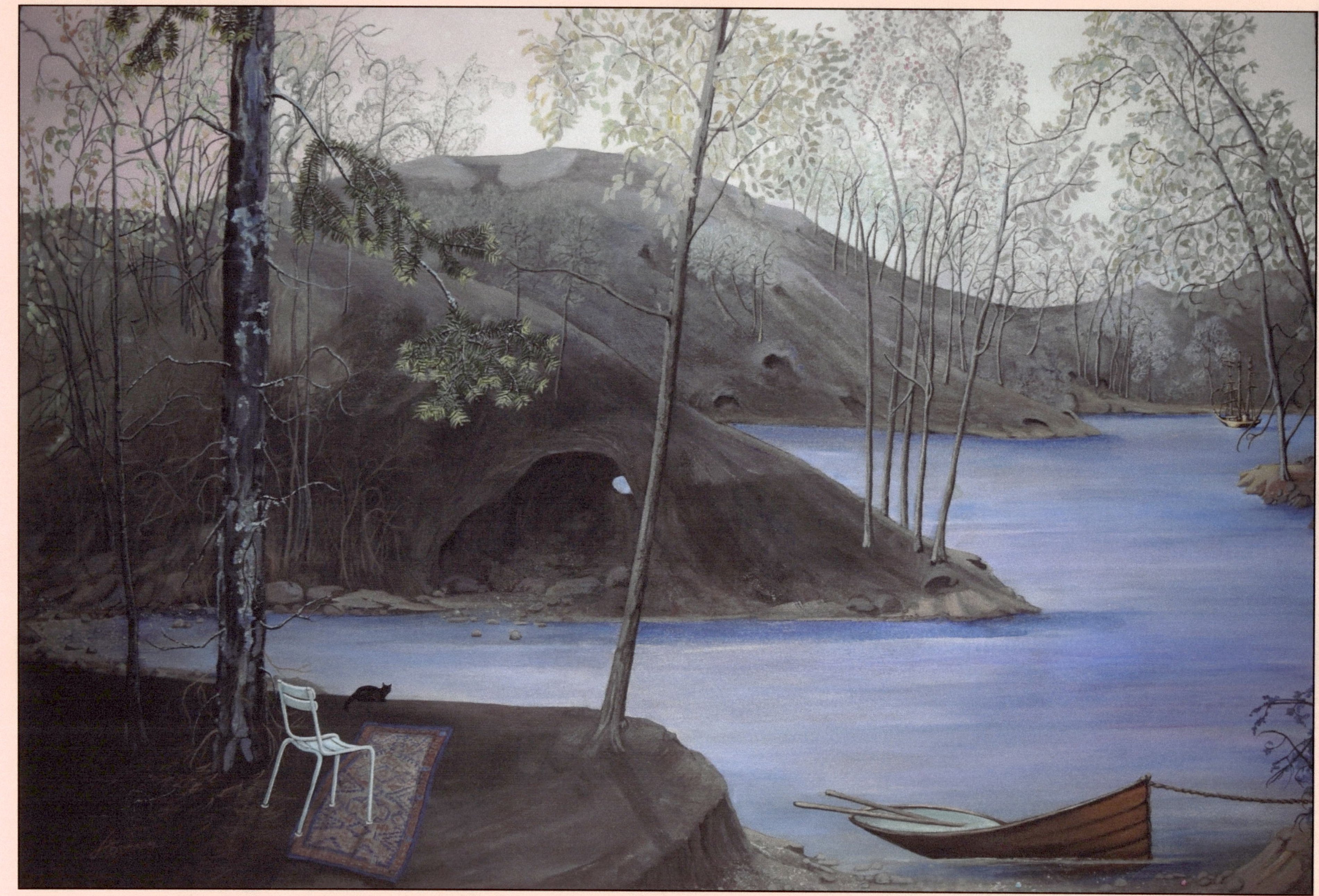

My Pirate Life

# My Pirate Life

If I was a pirate, I know where I'd stay;
in my Victorian house on my hidden cave bay.
The beach would be rocky; not so much that I'd wobble.
At low tide, if lucky, I'd find a gemstone or bauble.
My first mate (well, not quite) will serve Asian take-out and pie,
and would alarm me if a visitor comes by.

I'd go searching for treasures like antique chairs,
Oriental carpets and porcelain wares.
Eight pieces no worry; I'd be in no hurry.
A warm breeze smooth upon me I'd lounge by the sea,
with my cats softly furry and a Long Island iced tea.

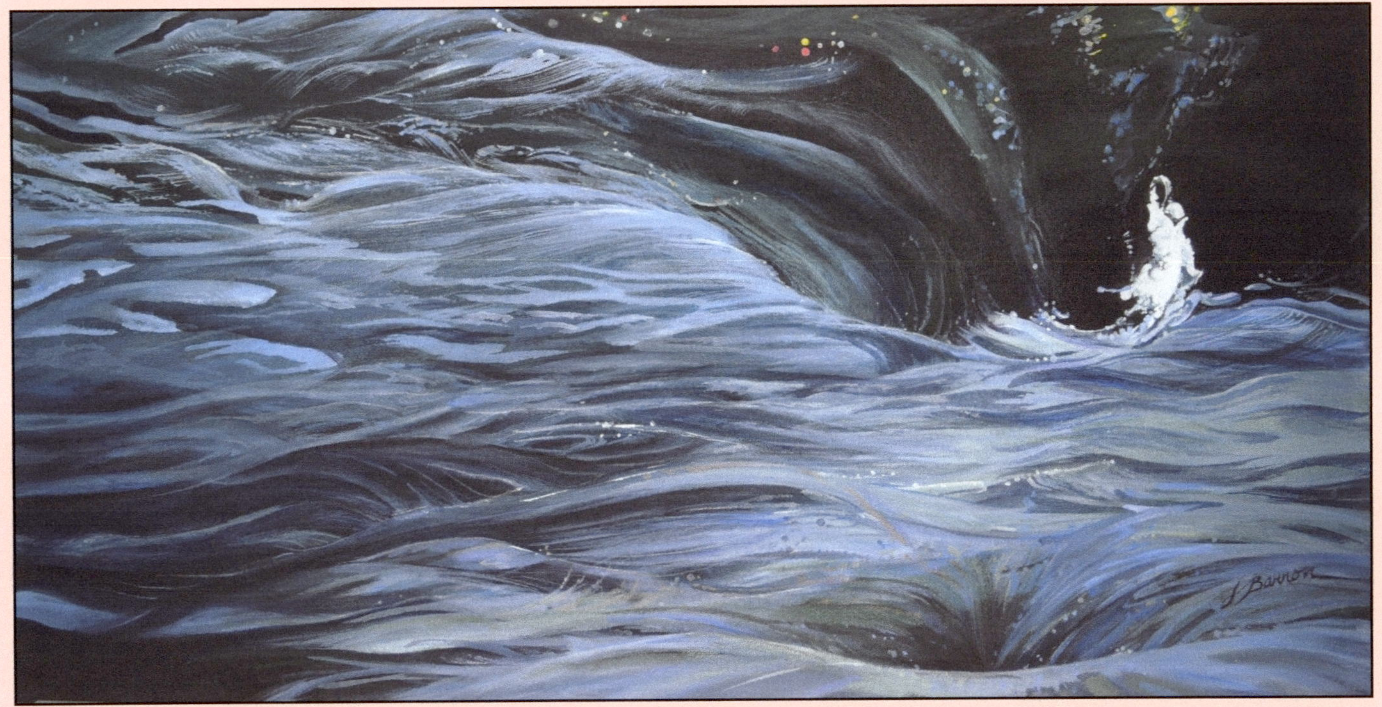

**Wave Warrior**

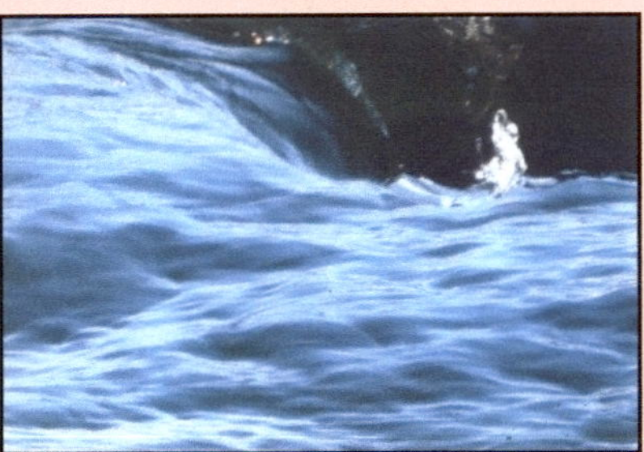

Insipiration photo taken from my boat on
Coeur d'Alene Lake.

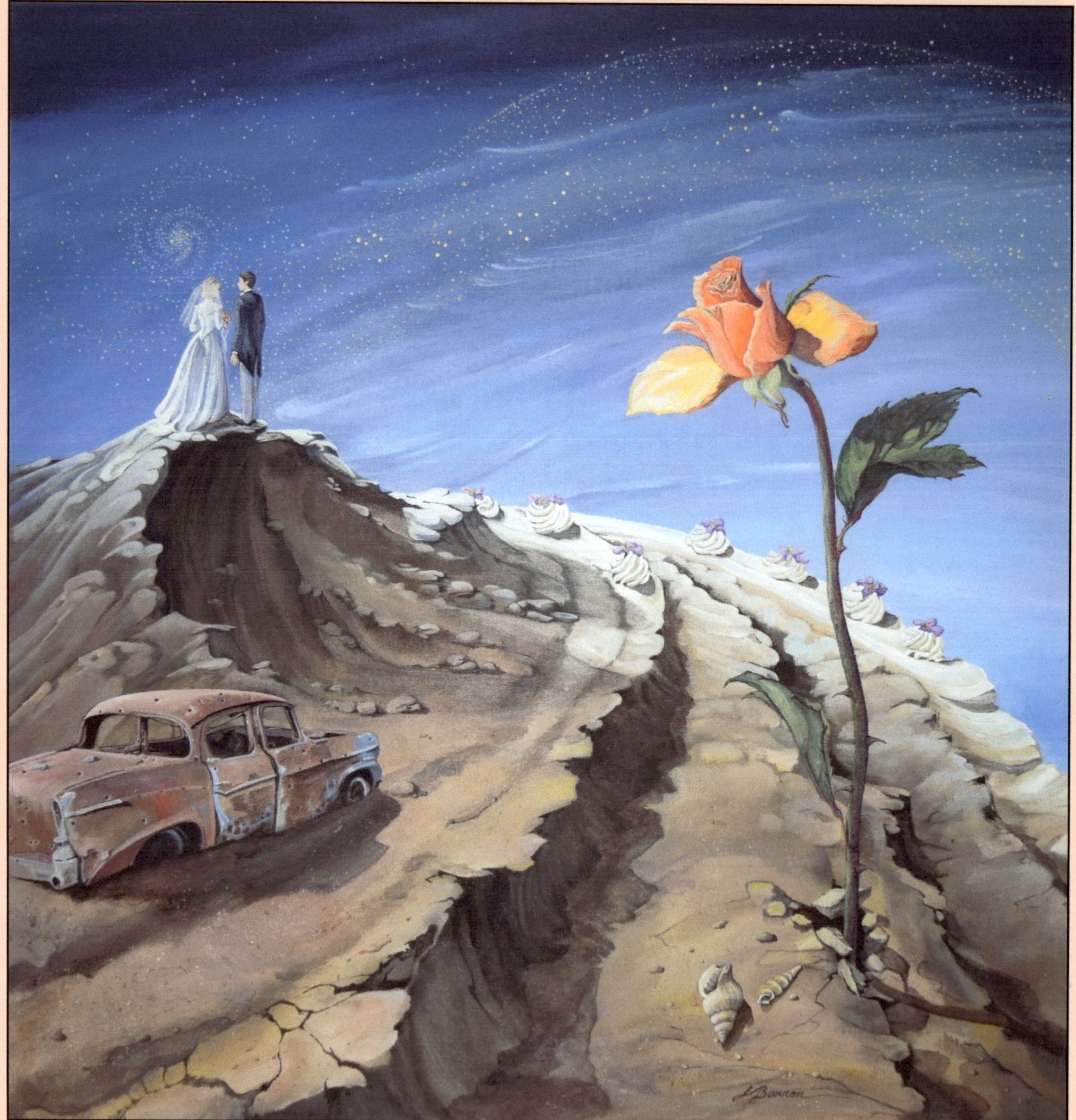

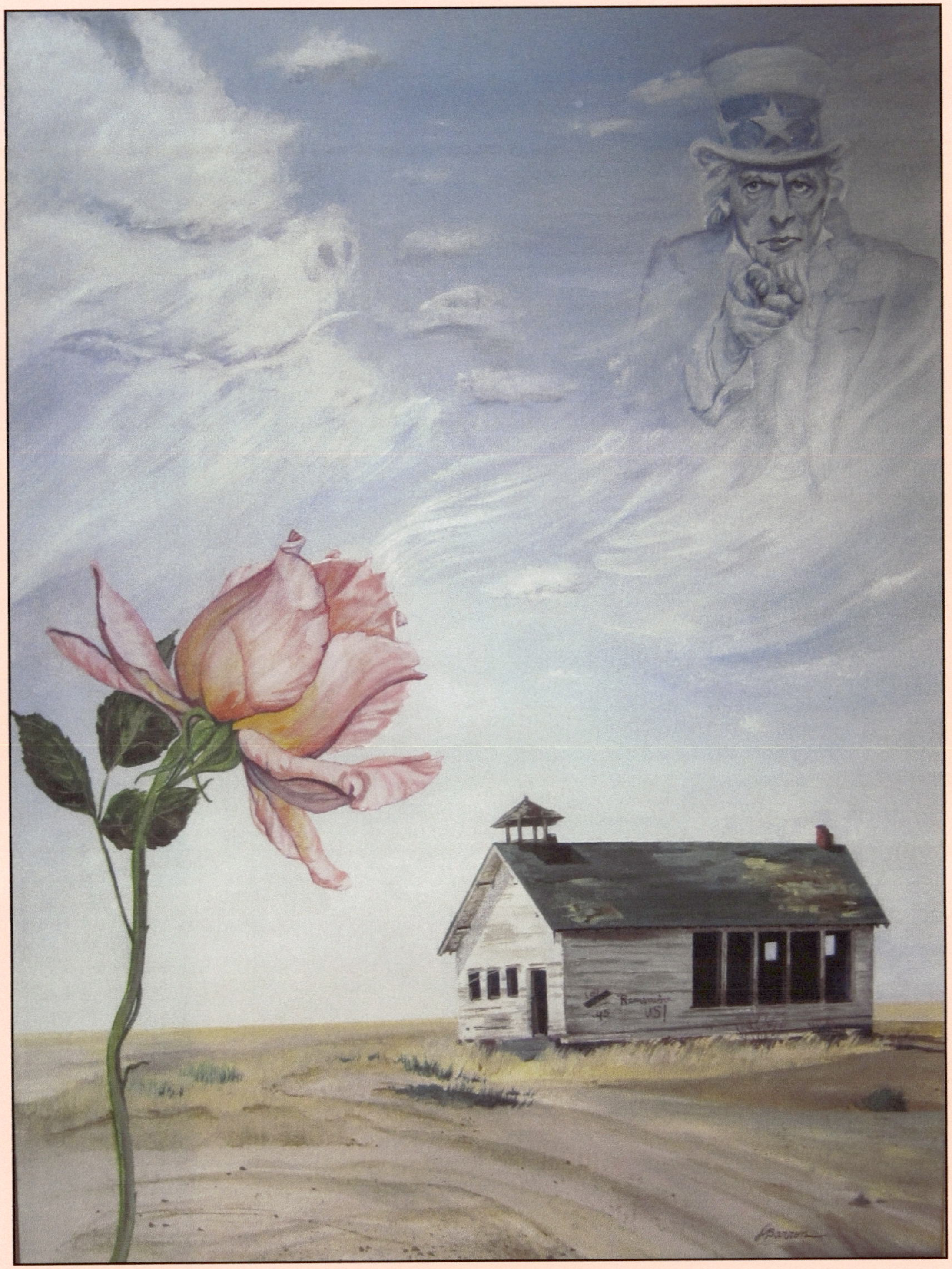

Remember Us

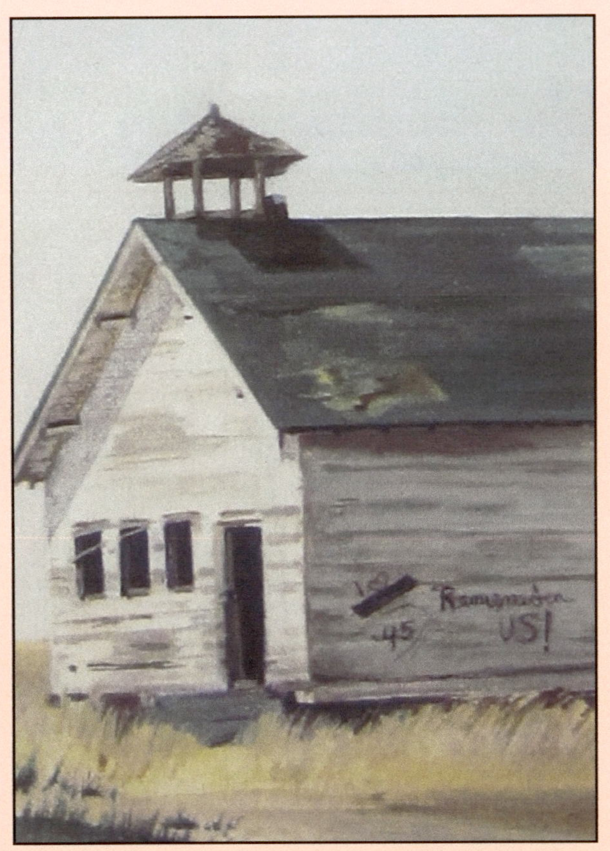

Detail

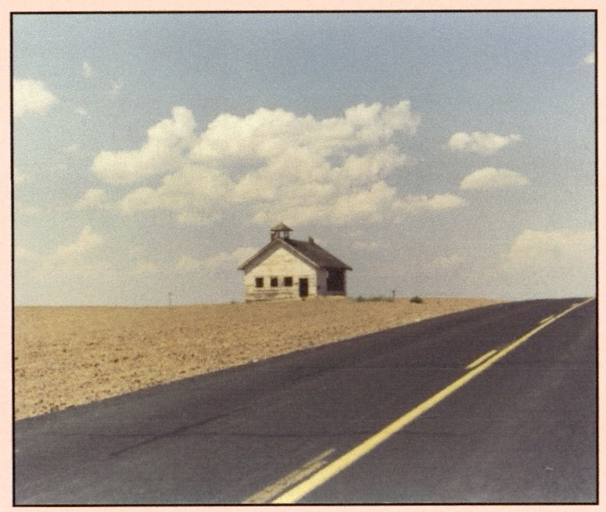

Inspiration photo

47

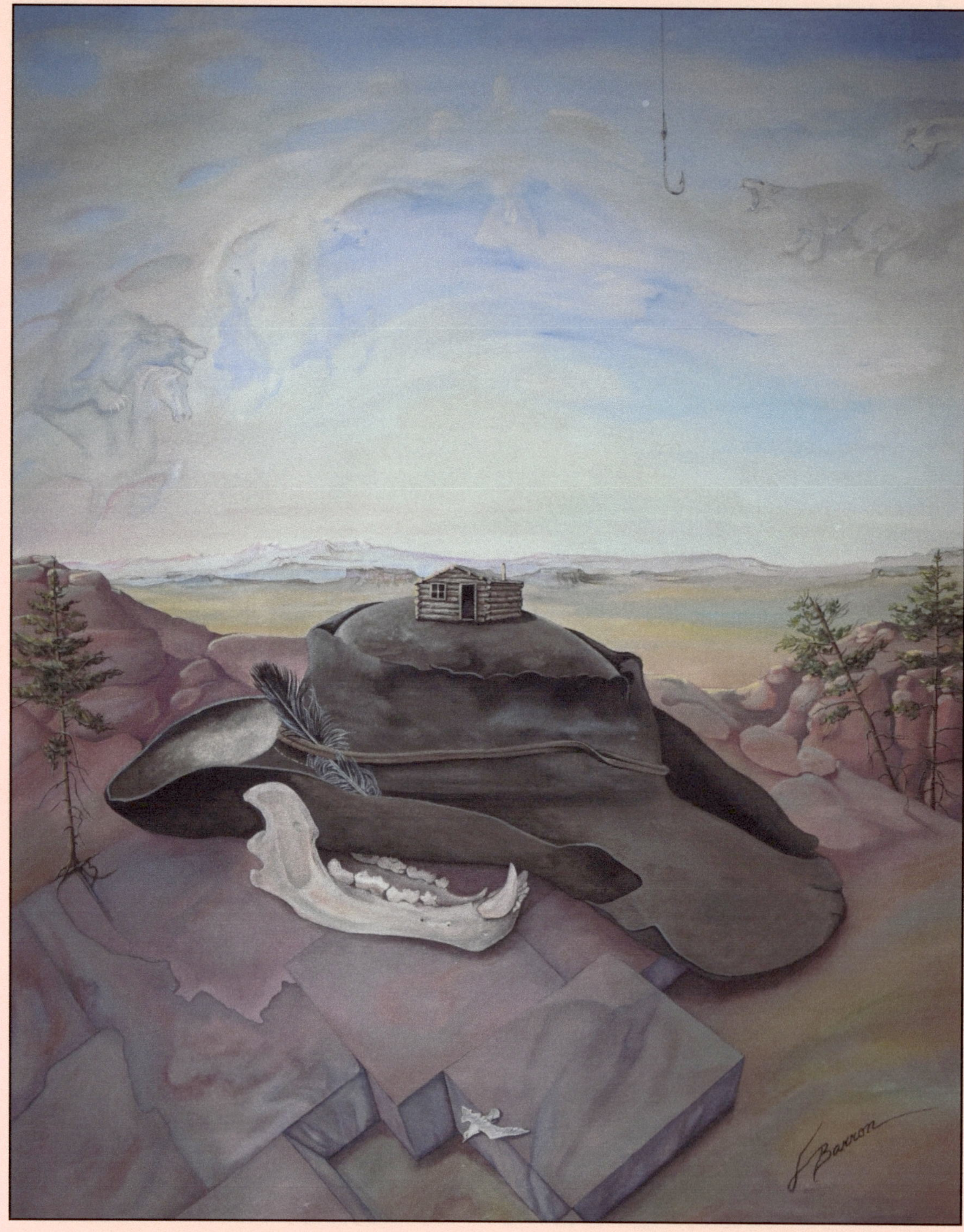

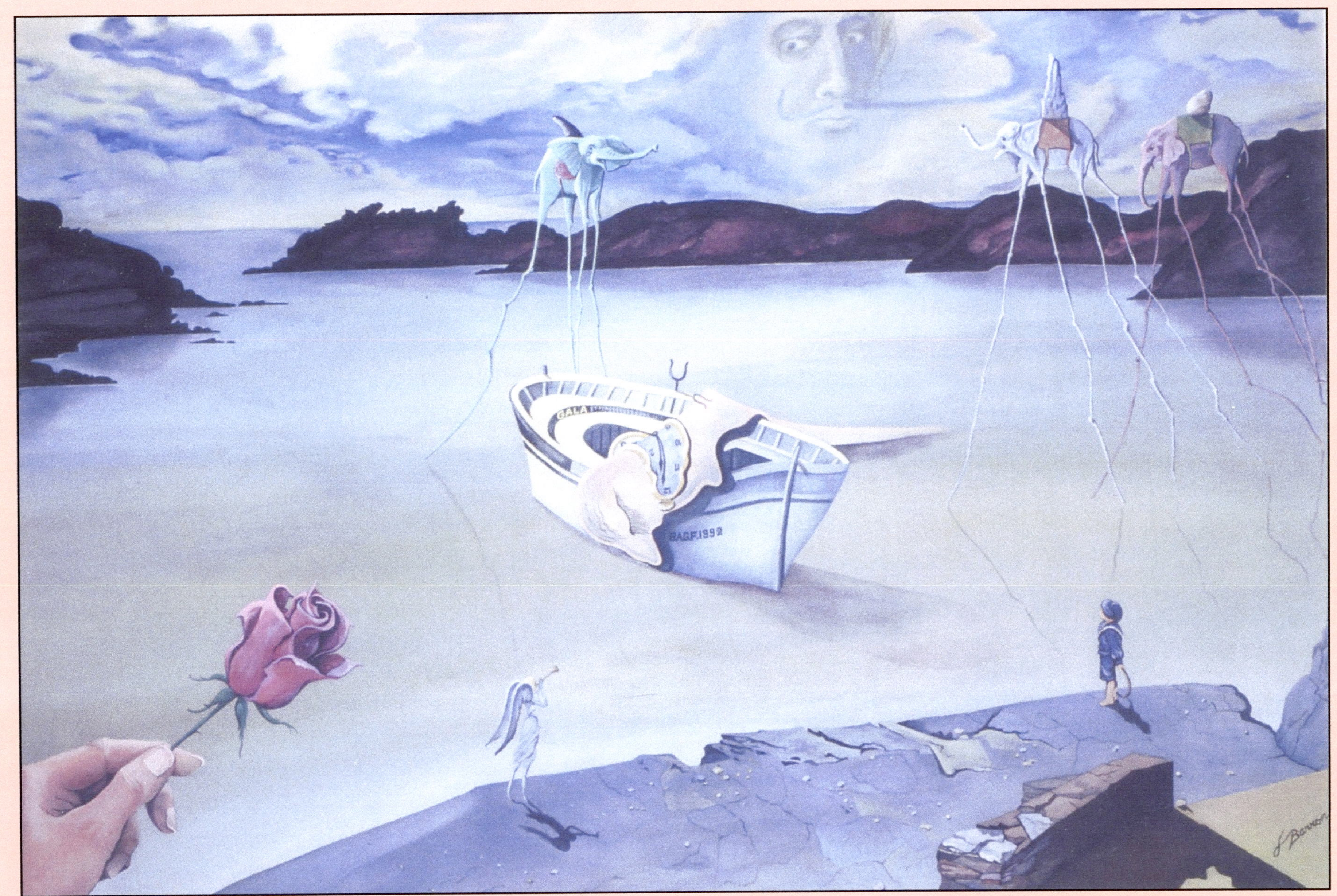

**Death of Dali**

# Swamp Gas My Ass
(1966)

I was a lass of seventeen,

but knew exactly what I'd seen.

It was truly very near,

not far away as painted here.

Through the window by the couch;

many others quick to vouch;

a silver orb of great dimension,

not an earthly air invention,

descended to the hidden lake;

a mental picture all to take.

News stories gave it a pass;

"swamp gas my ass."

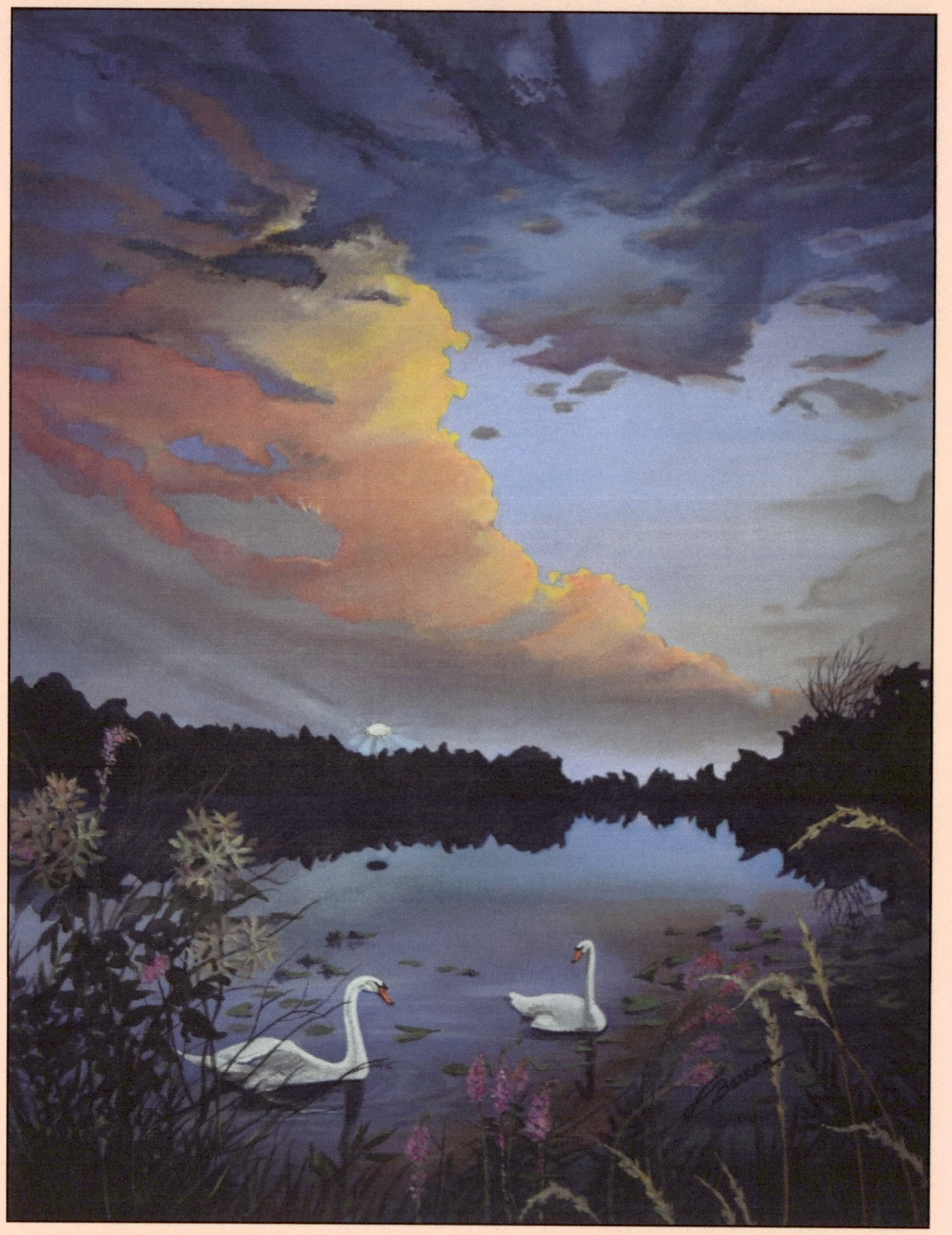

**Swamp Gas My Ass** | from Mom's millpond

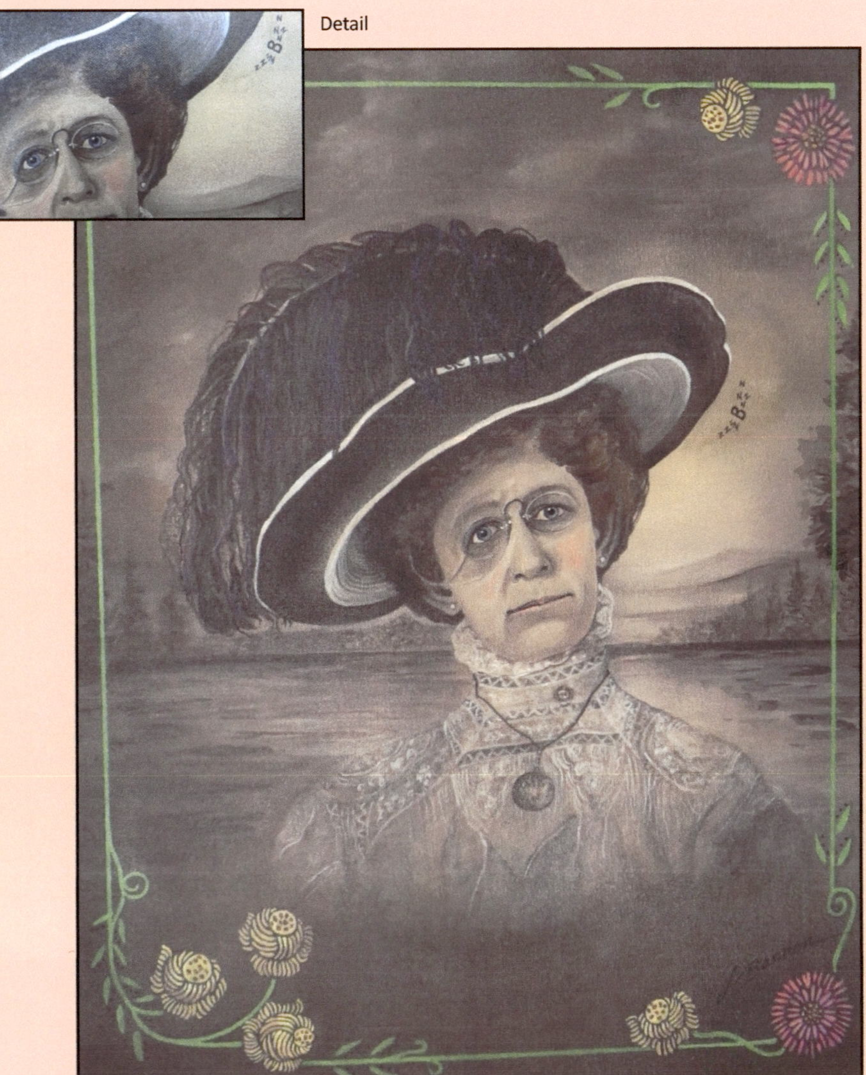



**Aunt Anna Oakley** | My Mother's friend, Vina, gave me this photo. As she was adopted, she wouldn't claim this lady as a blood relative...this sister of her adoptive grandmother. I'm not claiming her either.

# Aunt Anna Oakley
*(about to have a bee in her bonnet)*

A photo was decades stored away.

Gifted to see the light of day,

painted here for some to see,

was Great Aunt Anna Oakley.

You can't make up a name like that.

Imposing in her Victorian hat,

taller yet with ostrich plume,

suitors gave her ample room.

A bee is hovering rather near.

It will enter her bonnet I fear.

The spinster sister she remained;

nothing more to be proclaimed.

I imagine she liked cats and books;

tolerated sideways looks.

On Sunday she would sit in back.

Buying quality was her knack.

She traveled on a knowledge quest;

on holidays was a valued guest.

A suffragette, she marched the street,

the kindest person one could meet.

# Food is Fun

Food is fun when you control it;

smear it, roll it, even throw it,

slap it, squish it or un-dish it.

It can entertain you a long while.

Some will make it through your smile.

You enjoy the taste sensation;

another sense...a revelation.


Adults just play a different way;

a bit more subtle shall we say?

A triscuit directionally must be chewed,

with the grain lines or it's skewed.

By color there's the candy corn.

Some breads are better if they're torn.

Popcorn...cloudlike shapes you're shown.

Peanut shells in bars are thrown.

With barbeque you make a mess.

With caviar most can only guess.

Some foods earn a sigh in savor,

to announce delight of flavor.

Some people are "stir it" crazy,

or wolf it down ...they're never lazy.

Yes, food can be satisfying fun,

with every bite until there's none.

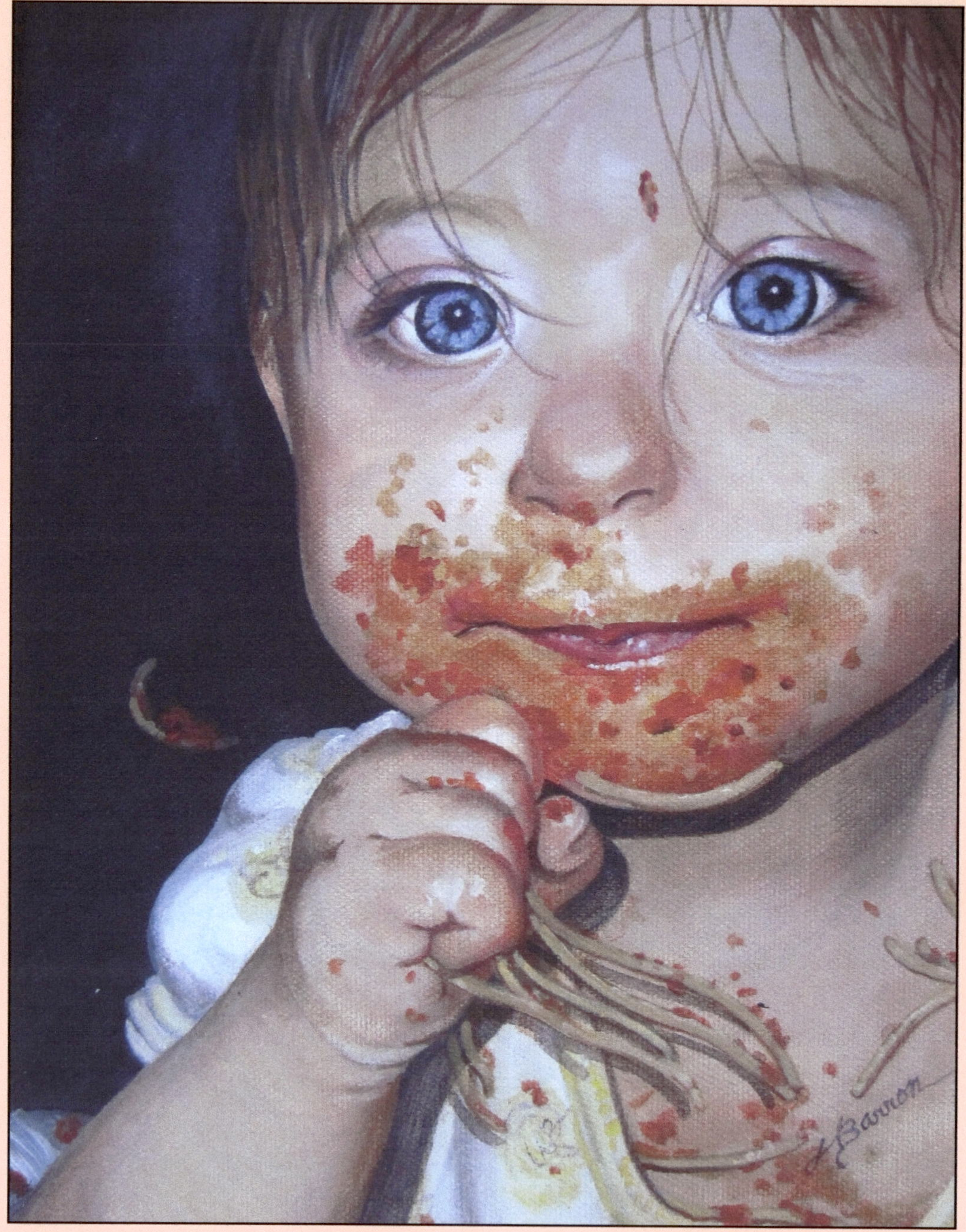

Food Is Fun

# Moose on the Loose

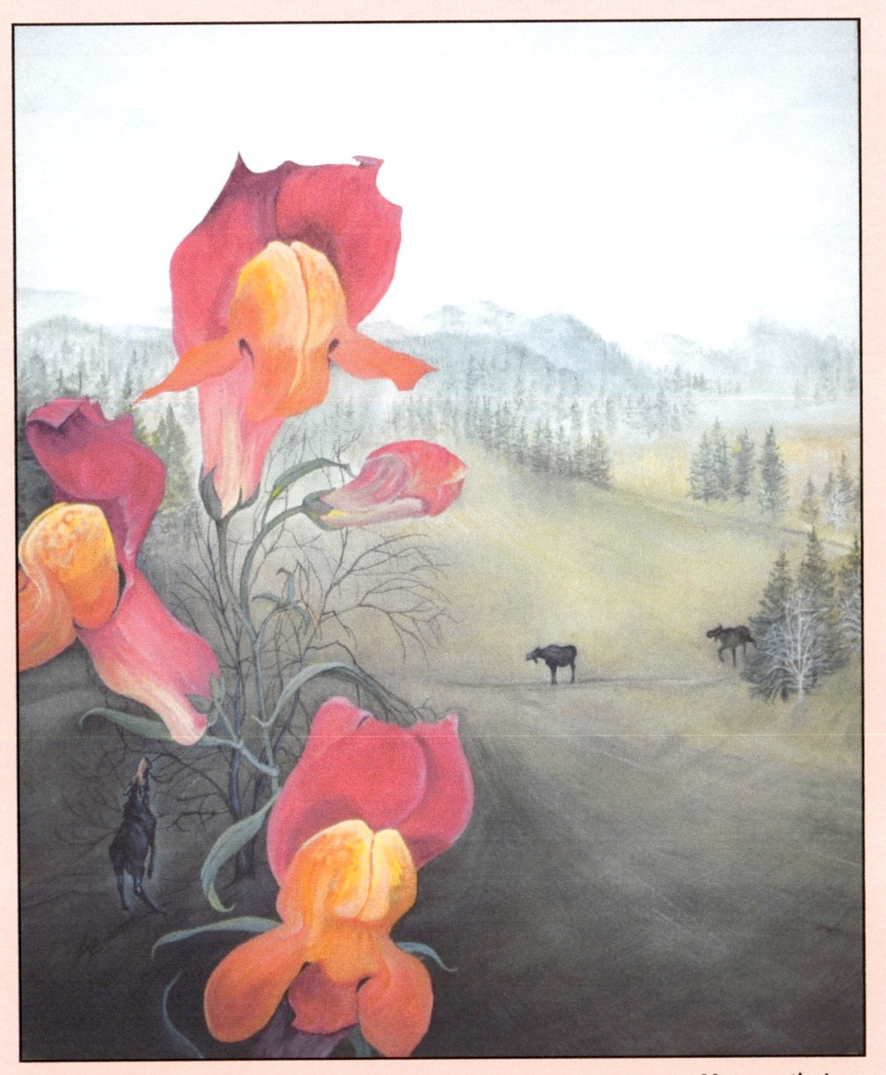

Moose on the Loose

One mouse is a mouse, and more are mice.

One moose is a moose, and more are moose.

It wouldn't be right to use that mice word twice.

If there was a threesome they could be called "thrice."

There's a moose on the loose on Loose Moose Loop.

The drive is called that as he often drops p_ _p.

Today he has company.  Yes, there are three;

more to munch on every tree.

The one that follows, or brings up the rear, could be called the

caboose...confusing?  Oh dear!

Though related to the deer...one is a deer and more are deer...

this is one animal to never go near.

They are enormous creatures, with strange awkward features.

With bulbous snouts, rounded antlers, and legs that are lanky,

they run about with dispositions quite cranky.

Watching them from afar is fun, but soon their visit will be done.

Their territory does abound, and they aren't ones to stick around.

Goodbye you moose. One, two and three...you moose caboose.

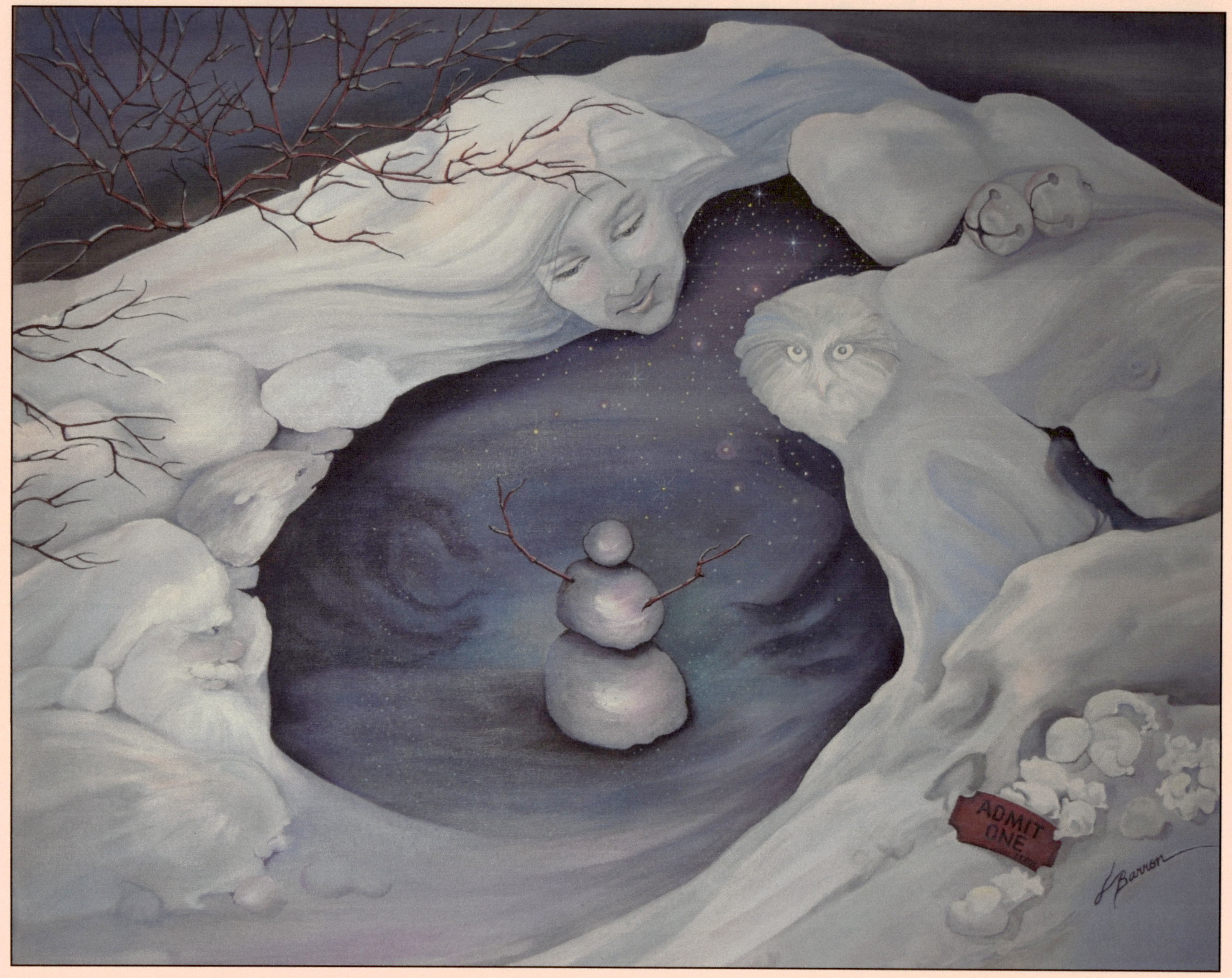



**The Snowman's Debut**

# The Snowman's Debut

Come one come all to the snowman's debut...

debut because he is brand new.

The children placed him in their little snow cave,

and stuck his stick arms in a welcoming wave.

Did he conduct from his place in the hollow,

all the magic that soon was to follow?

Fanciful faces appeared in the snow;

faces of those who had come for the show.

Snow fell and stars flowed and the snowman just glowed.

Like a puppet he stood there

(he can't move, he just stands),

but if you look closely you'll see puppeteer hands.

What happens next is for all to come see,

because after dark admission is free.

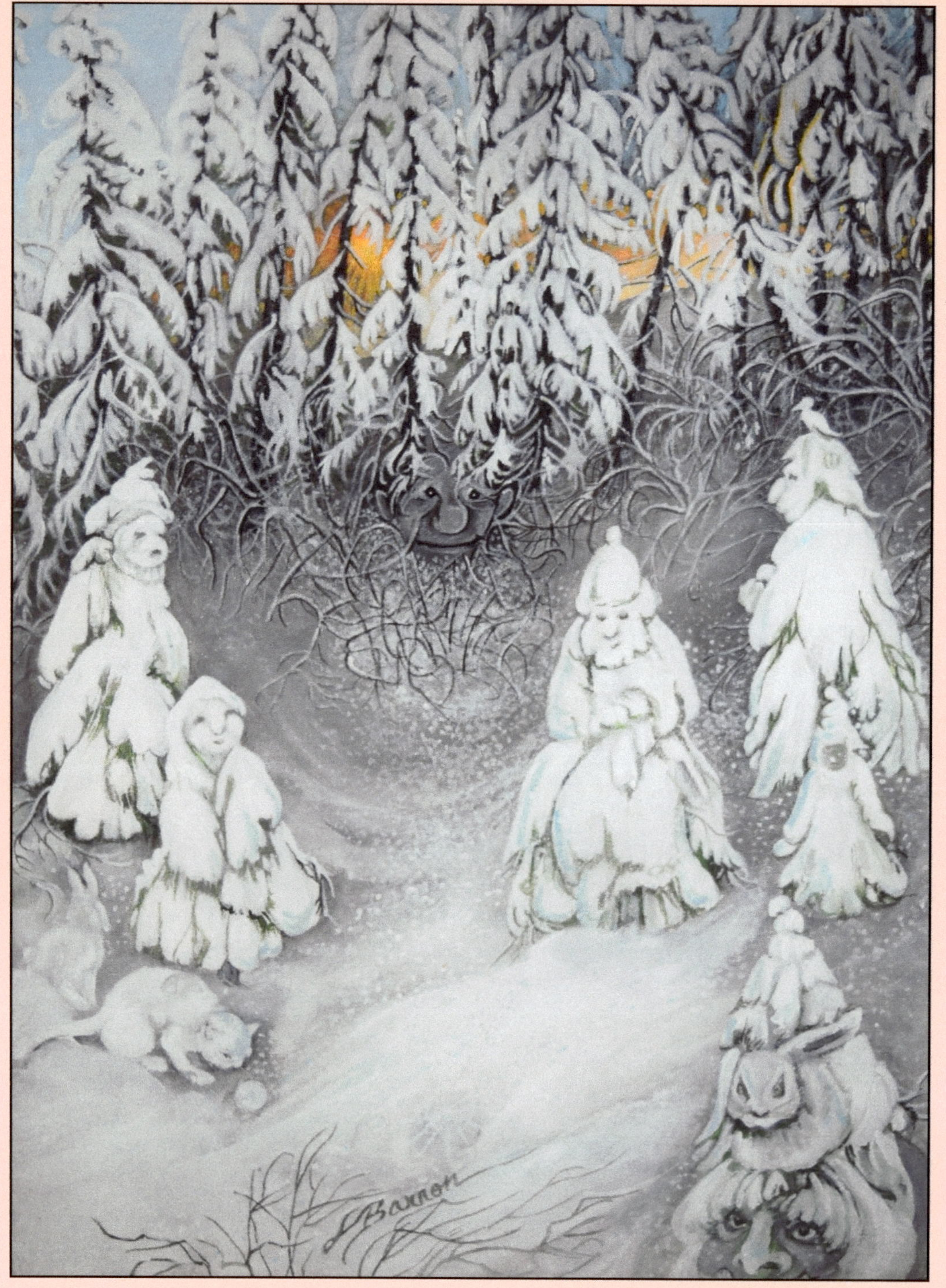

# Little Trees

Little trees are strong one knows,
to stand and carry heavy snows
that bend their tips so tiny
and load their branches piney.
They look like gnomes or elves,
and really not much like themselves,
with pointy hats and long white cloaks
they really are the cutest blokes.

*Should they be marching, chanting, singing?*
*Should they be holding bells a ringing?*
In front of all their guardians towering,
shielding them as they are flowering,
someday they'll be ones so grand,
and they will give the helping hand.
"They have no hands." you quietly say,
and you are right, but this is play.

Imagination's quite okay...a tiny bit of any day.
A gust of wind, and it's quite bitter,
encircles like a scarf of glitter,
and seems to warm their sluggish sap.
I think it's time they take a nap.
They have been such fun to see,
we do not care what they will be.

---

# It Was Predicted... Snow Surprise

Snow snuck upon us all night long,
cloak of white hushed morning song.
Abruptly the view is concealed,
distant mountains unrevealed.
Sky a wall of milky haze,
colors vanquished to shades of grays.
Only one left to be seen...

peeks on pines in blackest green.
They line the drive now undercover,
imposing in a line they hover;
soldiers in torn drooping coats,
at attention high as the eye floats
to tiny burdened bowing heads,
bent to see us in our beds.

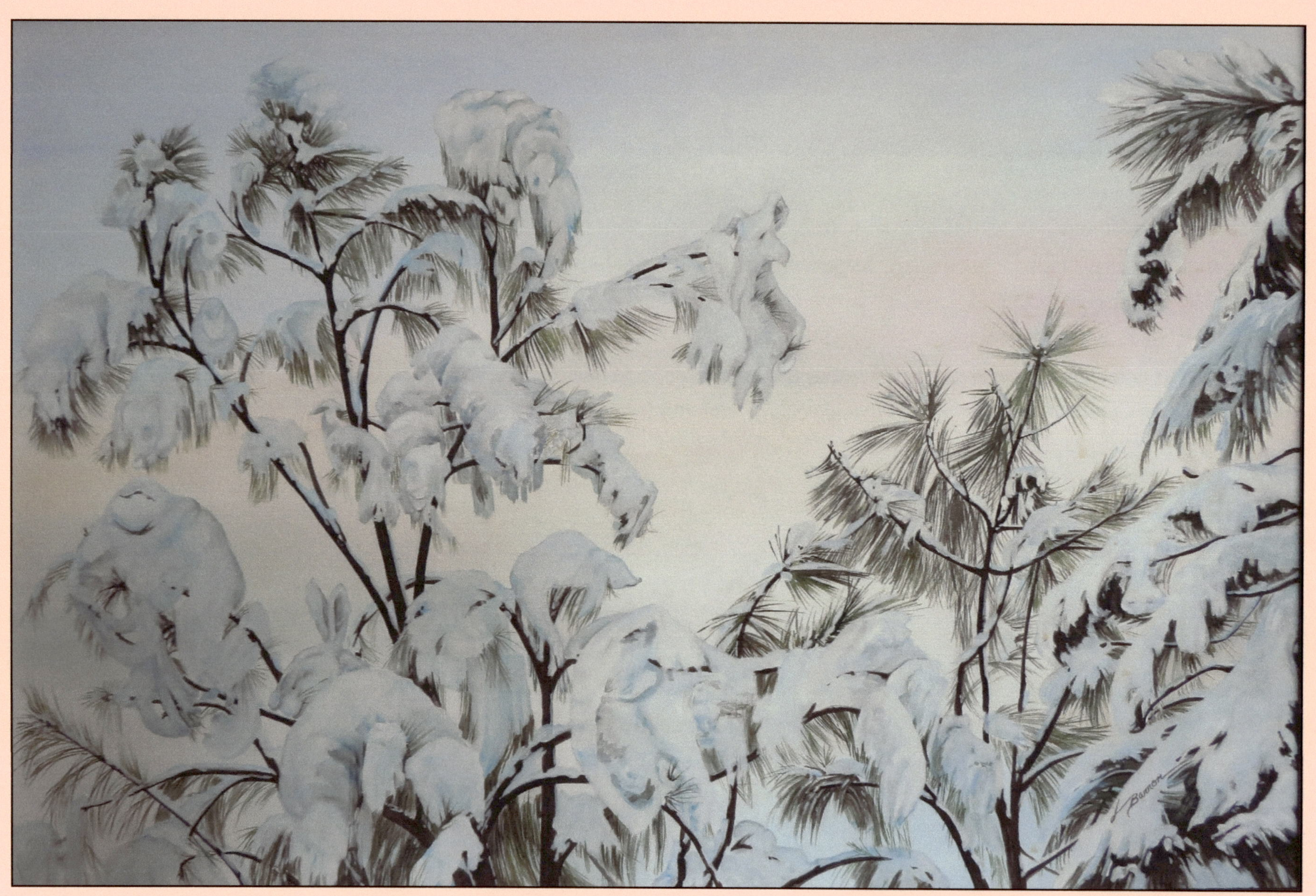

**Snow Critters on the Tree Tops**

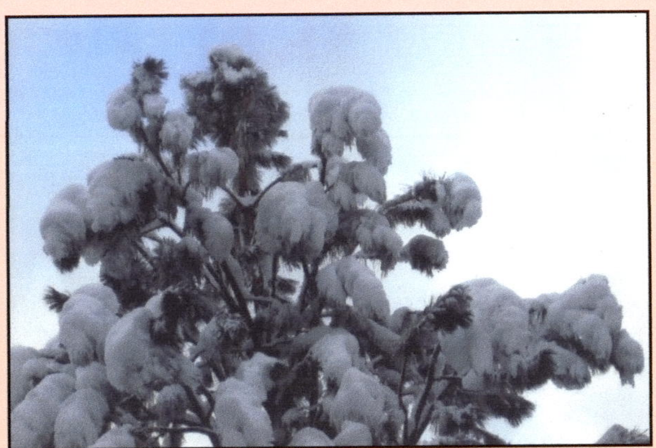

Inspiration for Snow Critters

# Snow Critters on the Tree Tops

It's stunning isn't it?...

the snow that softly falls all night

and you awake to the wondrous sight

of your whole world gone white.

Color has vanished from the scene,

all but the dullest and deepest of green

that accents each snow laden branch of the pines;

farther... all milky blurred are the lines;

sky, mountain and ground are all blended,

confusing where one begins or one ended.

Towering pines have their little heads bent

to see what wonders the night has sent.

The snow critters are back to play

until warmer weather sends them away.

On high branches they mingle,

these white fluffy creatures,

all with the most amazing of features.

*Monsters are crawling, bears are sprawling,*

*bunnies are running and birds are falling.*

Some are silly or scary or harder to find,

but it's nice to remember they're all from your mind.

You look up and you see them

in shapes and in shading,

but soon they'll be melting, and plopping and fading.

Fading back where they came from...up up and away...

you'll see them in clouds where they usually stay.

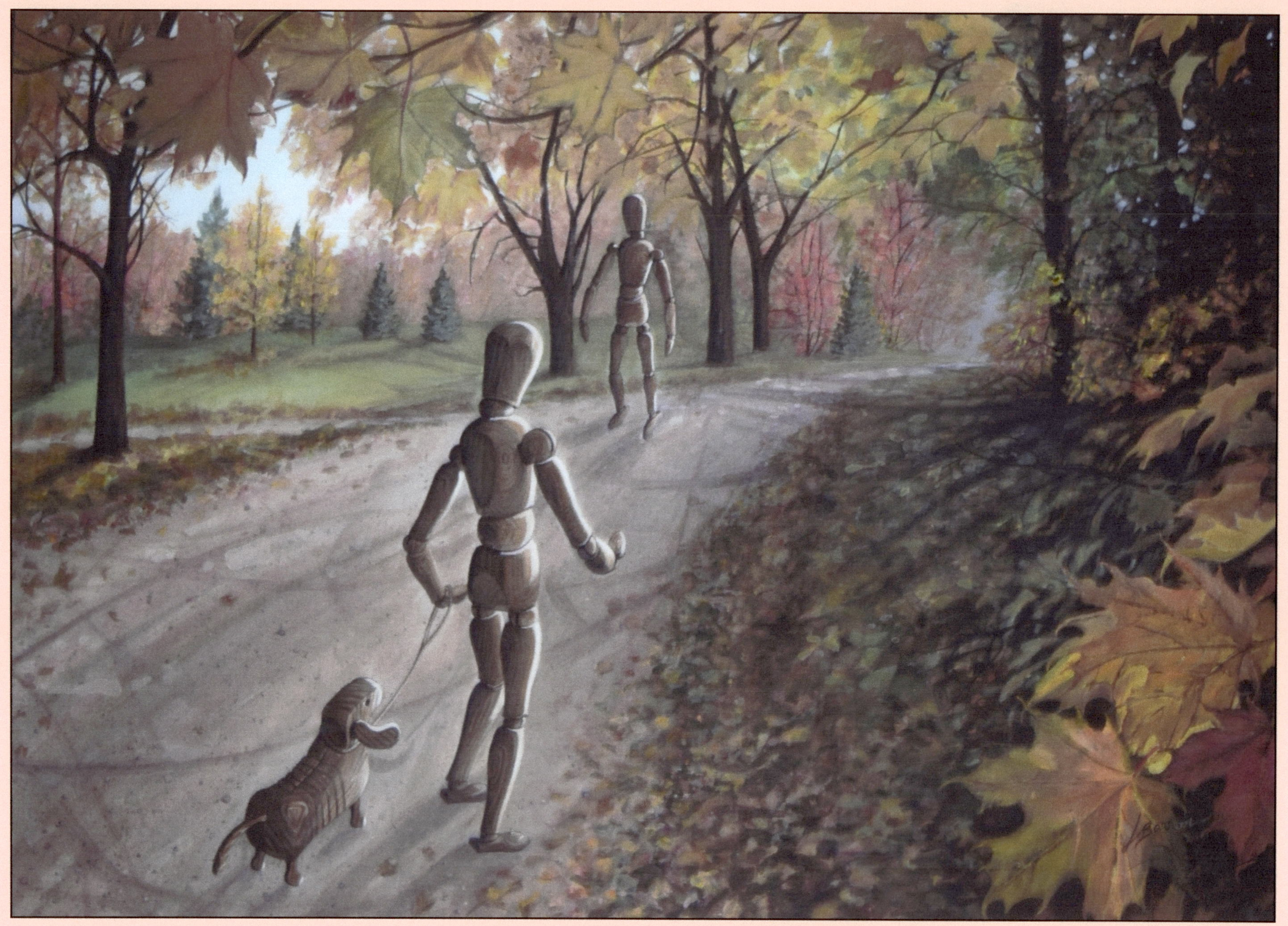

Shy Encounter

# Shy Encounter

They were quite young,

life just begun.

She thought of him both day and night;

his approach brought crippling fright.

Her instinct was to turn and run,

but then he'd know she'd come undone.

On needles did she slowly walk,

wishing they might finally talk.

Barely could she meet his eye,

and all that croaked a lonely, "Hi."

She knew he shared her admiration,

yet there'd be no proclamation.

So quiet and shy,

they'd just walk by.

She felt an intravenous weakness,

afflicted by her painful meekness.

Maybe fate knew something deeper;

he wasn't meant to be her keeper.

It would lead her other places,

through the grip of many faces.

Sometimes she'd float back to then,

dreaming of what might have been.

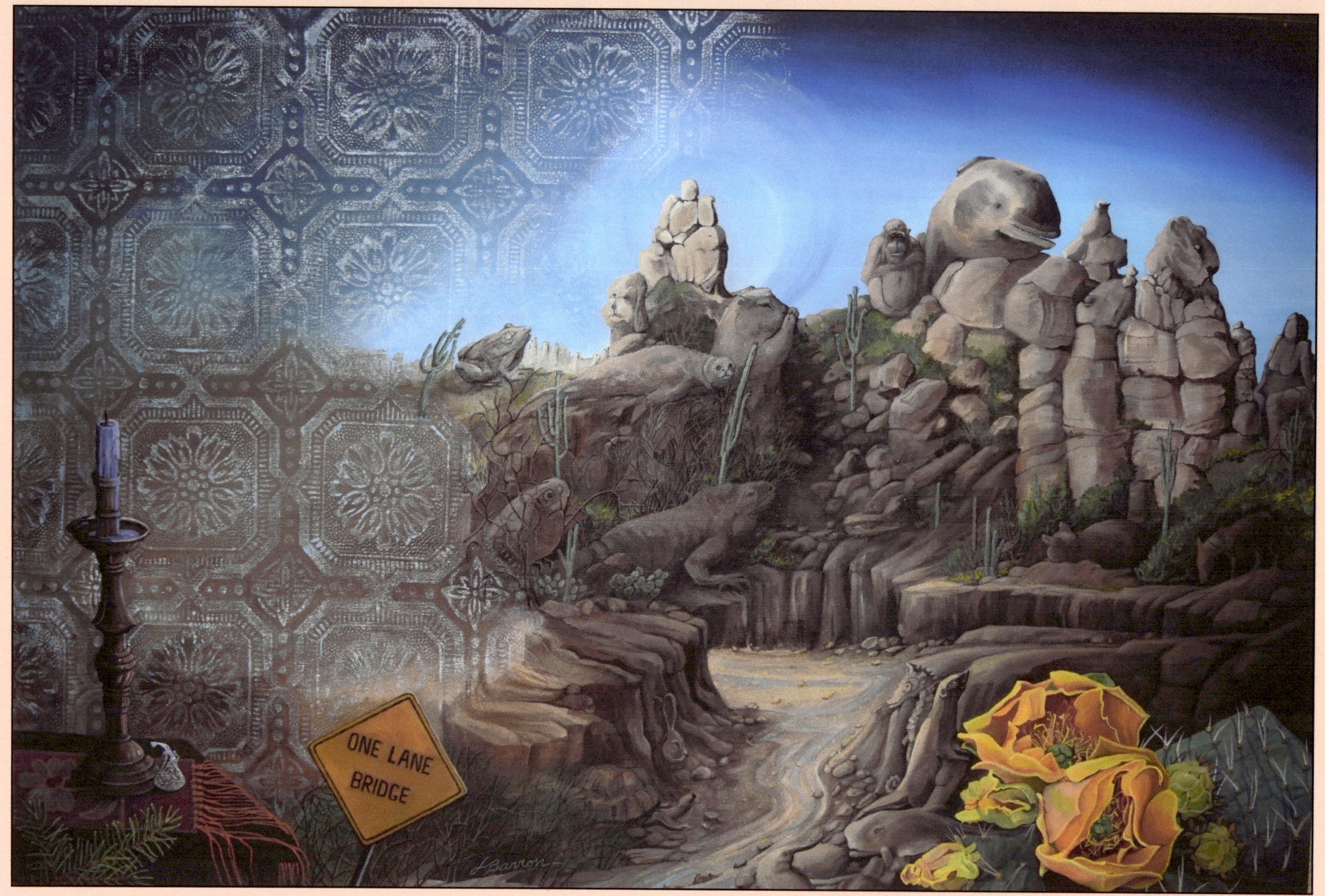



Arizona on My Mind

# After He Leaves

My house is full of empty beds.

Long corridors run from my head.

My house has another empty chair.

You are not there...you are not there.

You've gone ahead...you've gone ahead;

you've flown away to heaven's stead.

My house is full of empty chairs.

I purchase more to hold my cares.

I have your toys in a closet deep,

and memories I'll always keep.

Uncomplaining throughout "no cures";

you showed us how a man endures.

The dew has turned from diamonds to tears;

washed away your discomfort and fears.

You had to go...you had to go;

the morning sun does tell me so.

I'm not alone...you're not alone;

for in my heart you have a home.

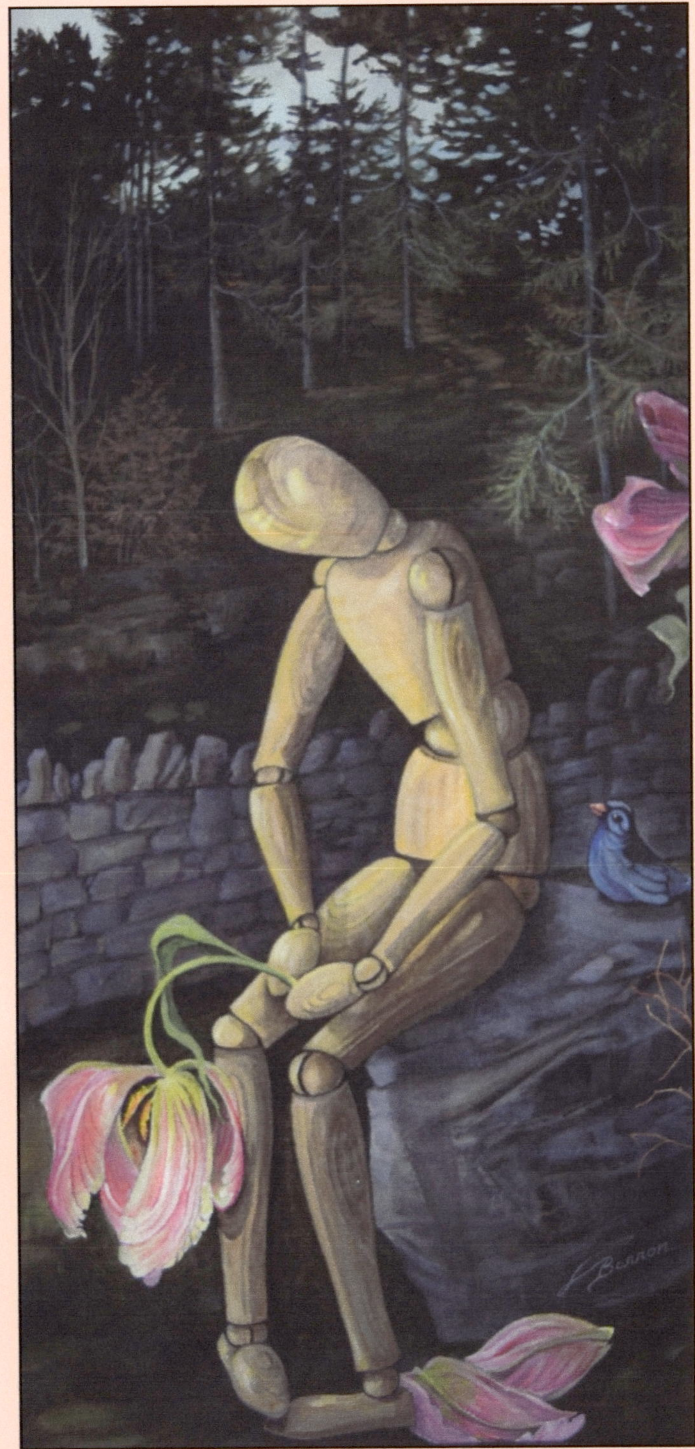

Holding on to Beauty

# IV. Of Farms & Barns

## The Developer

Nobody's worked harder than the farmer next door.

No one left to till his ground anymore?

He's grooved it like a fine tooled leather;

prayed over it during inclement weather.

His money is in his land.

He's loved that land…you understand.

He deserves to finish his life,

in comfort without guilt or strife.

Who buys large acreage now;

if not to love and not to plow?

Beauty being chipped away,

and yet we knew it wouldn't stay.

Out the windows that we lift,

nature has been a stunning gift.

Now more lights are in our view;

more houses, more people…nothing new.

YOU want to take another bite.

Crowd them in…we'll see the blight.

How much money need you make?

How many pieces must you take?

We don't endorse this work you do.

Then or again you're nobody new.

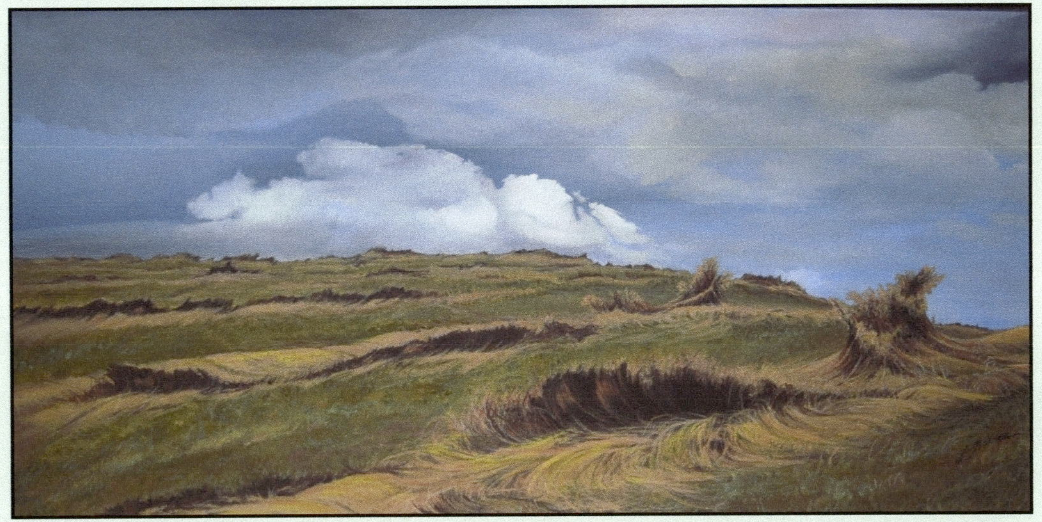

The Gleaning

# Flower Symbols

Flowers symbolize renewal or rebirth.
I entreat them with enormous girth,
showing them with a kingly worth.

They're nature's calming grace,
peace and beauty in any place.
This emphasis is quite my choice,
to give a painting stronger voice.

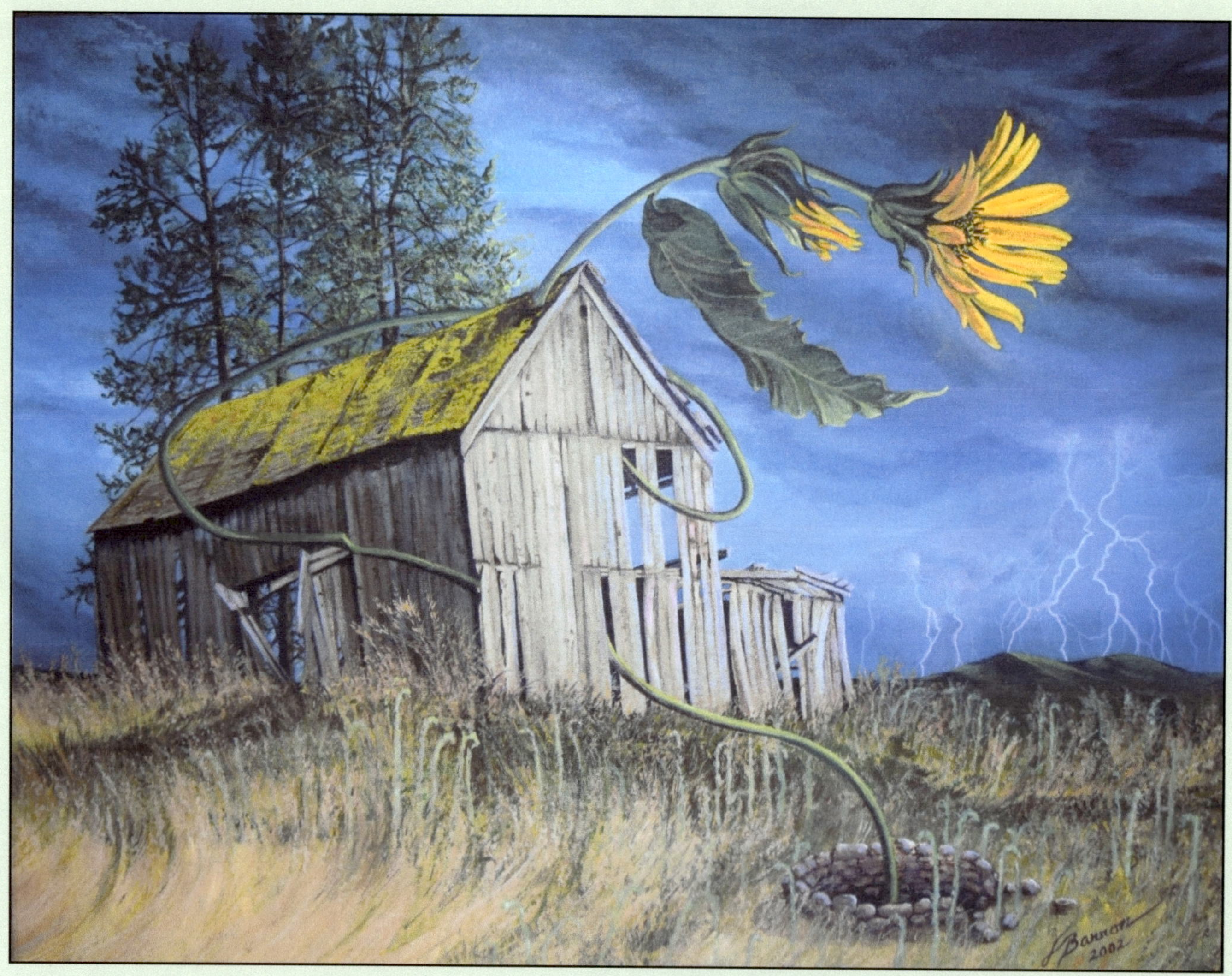



**Endurance**

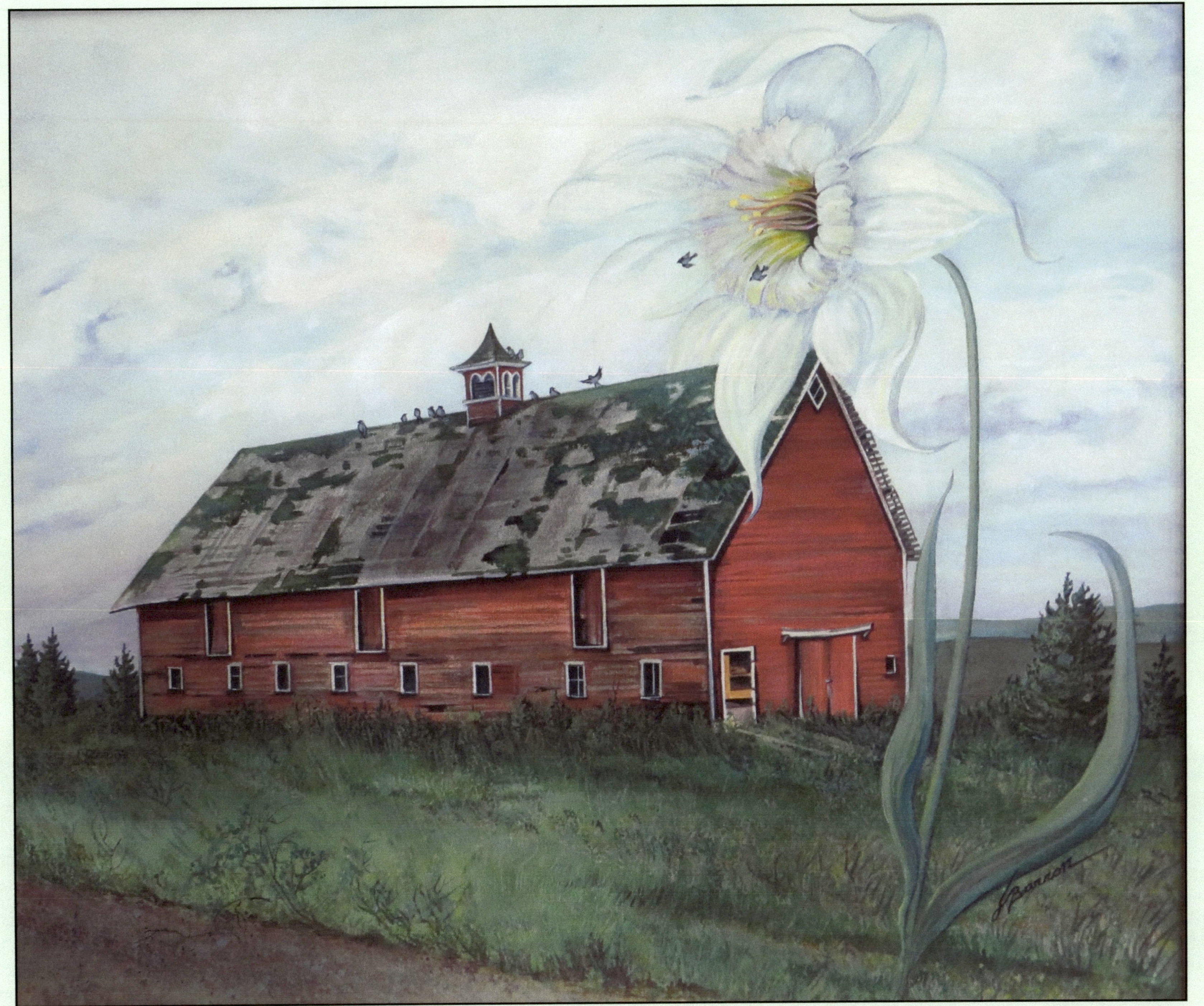

**Long Red Barn**

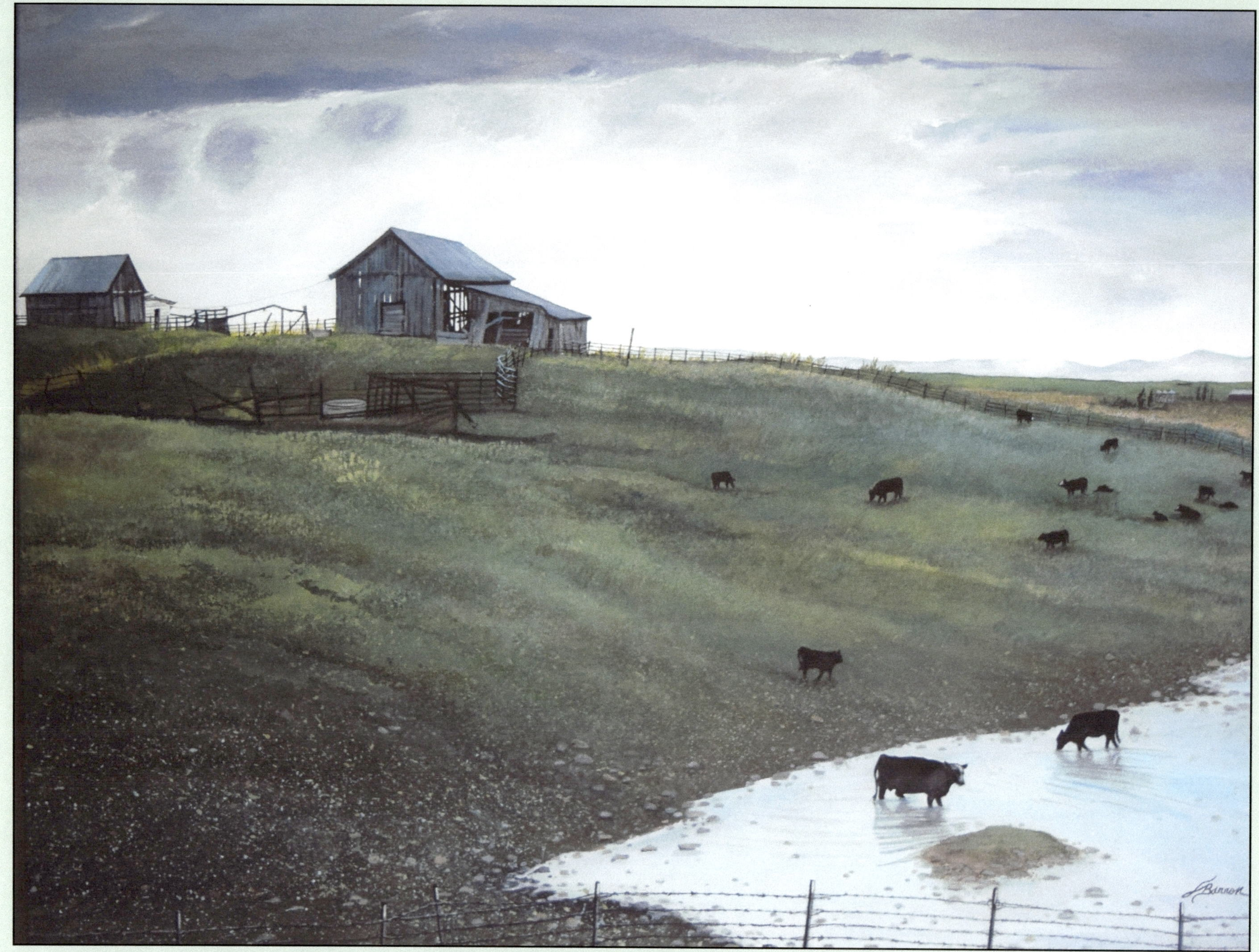

**Silhouettes**

# Silhouettes

Silhouettes against the sky,

caught my eye as we drove by.

Colors from the light of day,

slowly meld and fade away.

Dark clouds loom in evening's gloom;

swept by an invisible swirling broom.

In this passing quietude,

thoughts take a U-turn toward rude.

Munching cows of gentle disposition,

emitting a harmful gas composition?

Cow flatulence has become an issue.

Let me grab a facial tissue.

*Will I laugh or will I cry,*
*as I dab my wetting eye?*

Great herds of buffalo thundered the plain.

First golden arch...did grandmother complain?

I eat mine with ketchup and mustard.

The very thought must get you flustered.

Your shoe will never touch manure,

as you contribute to the city sewer.

Perhaps you'd better mask your rear...

that's your cloud in my atmosphere.

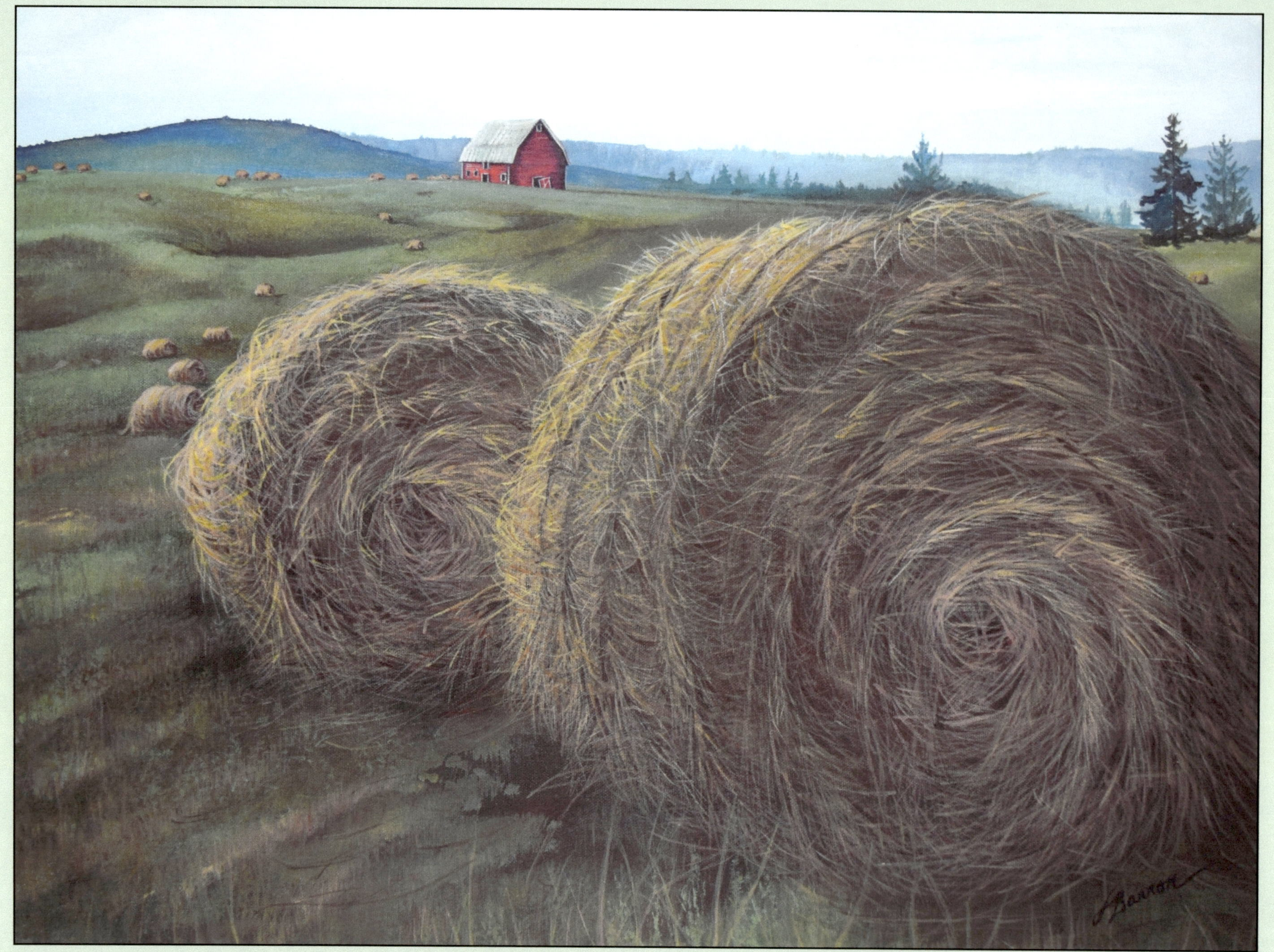

**Old Elephants**

HEALTHY FOOD
The
NEW
ERA
SCIENTIFICALLY
PROCESSED
POTATO
CHIPS

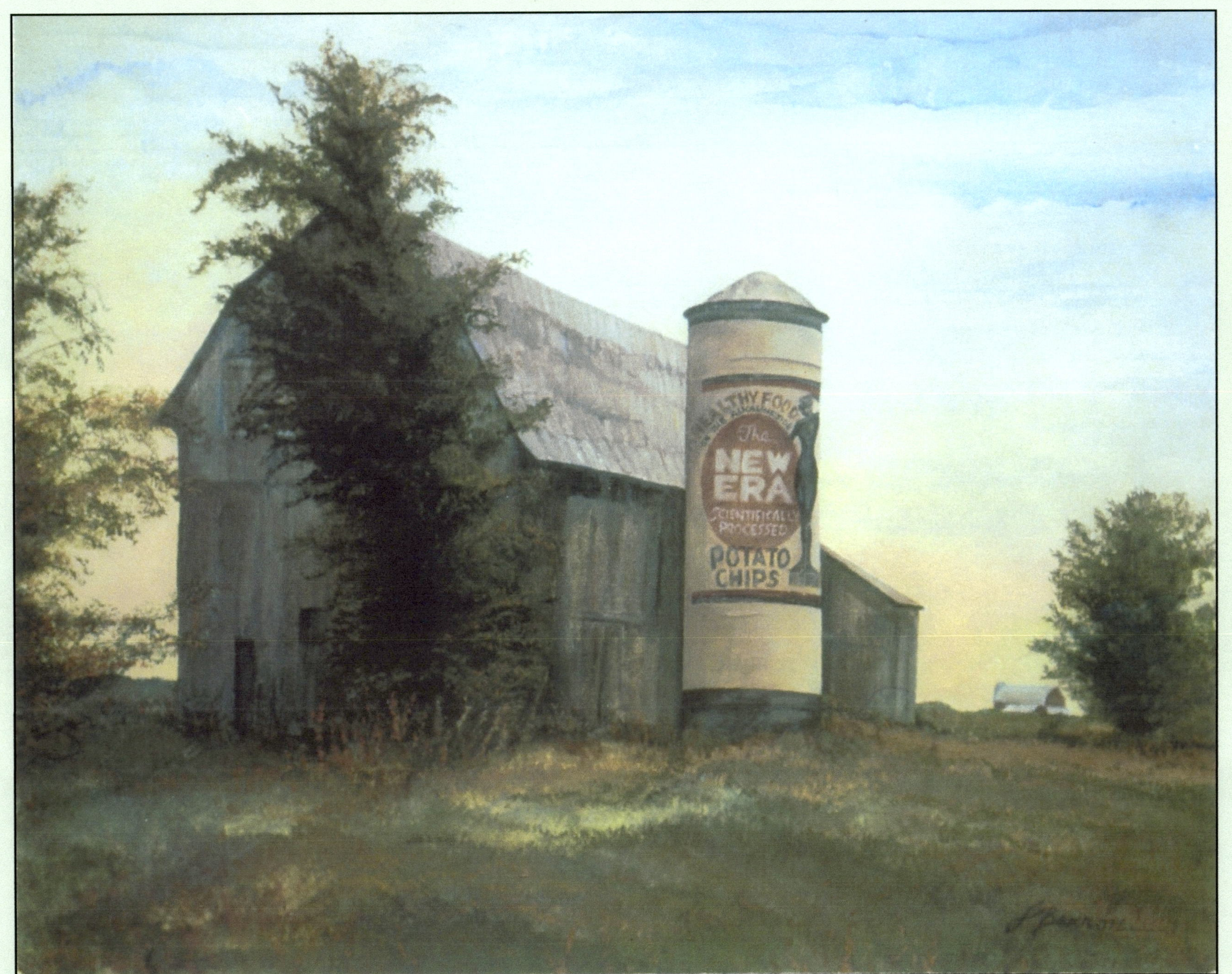

New Era 2000

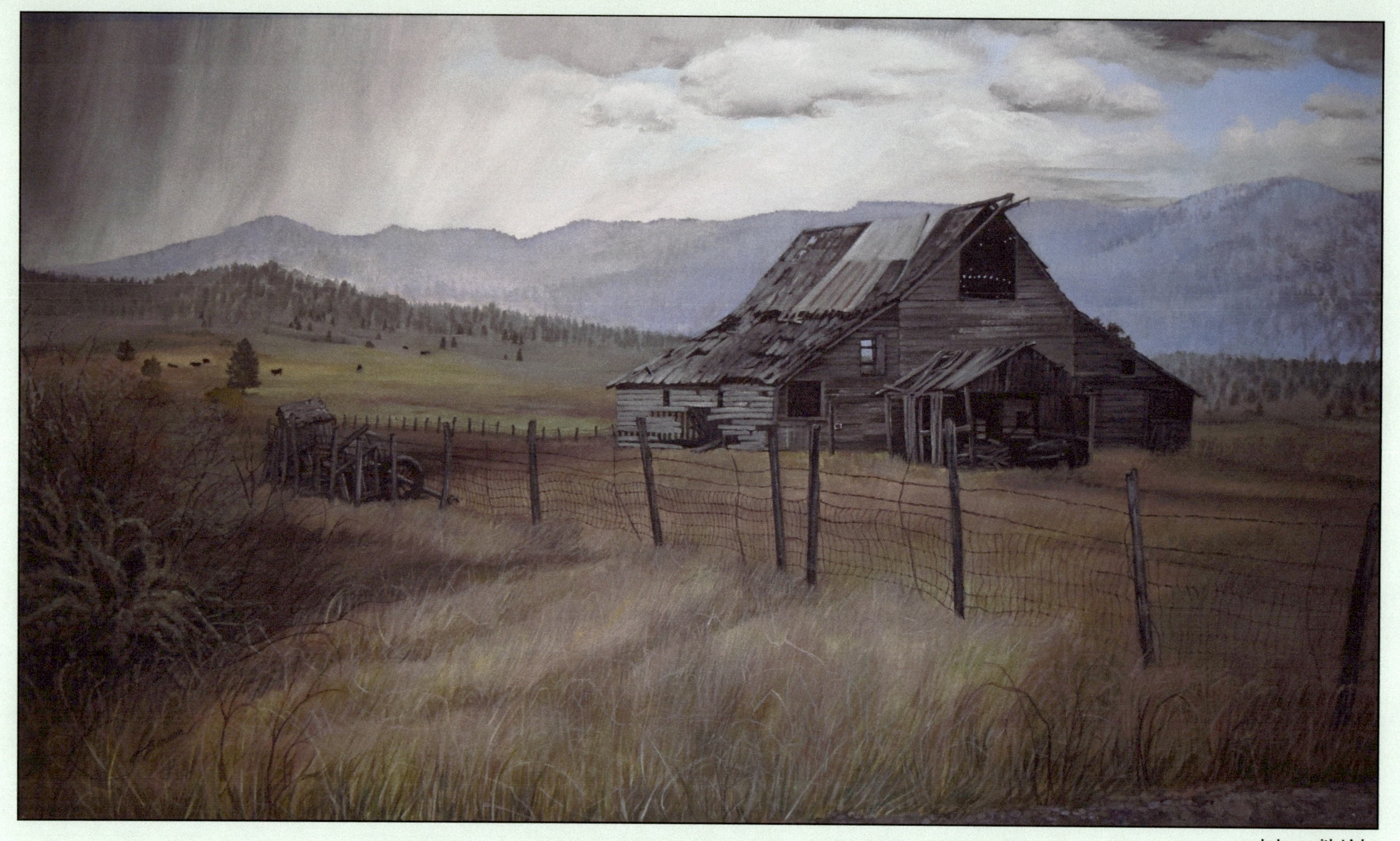

In Love with Idaho

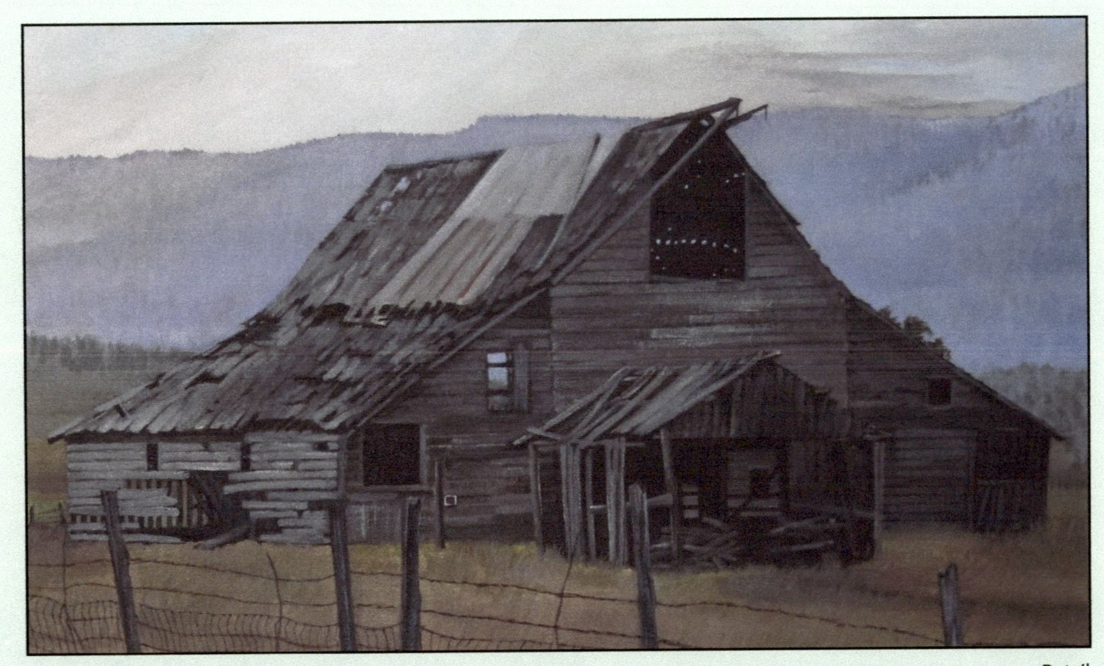

Detail

There's beauty everywhere, but Idaho is drenched with it.
There's serenity everywhere but Idaho enfolds you.
It whispers, "There now.  You are so fortunate to be here."

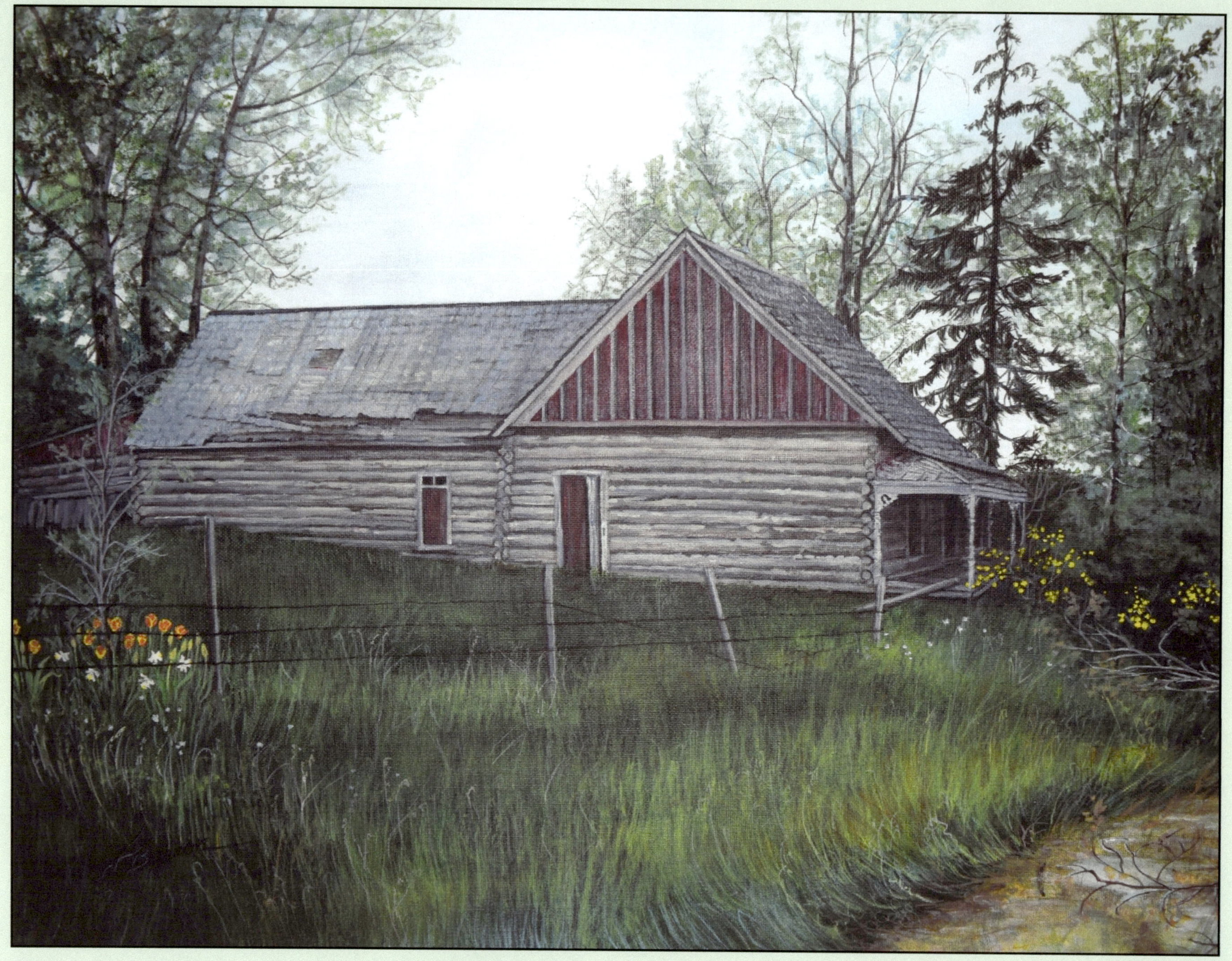

**Old Log Grange**

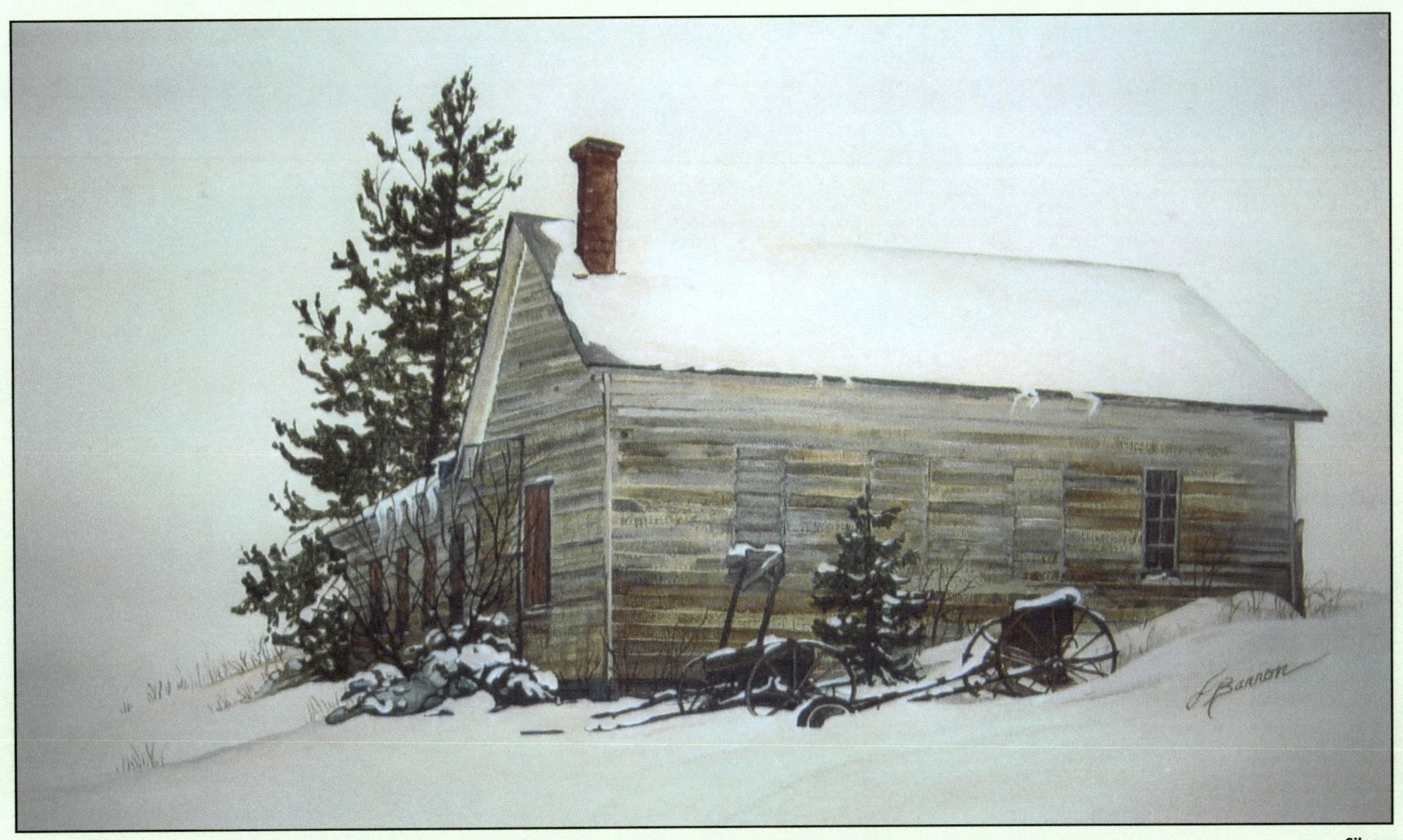



# The Grange Hall

The grange hall was a gathering place,
offering **belonging** in its space.
Farmers and members shared opportunity,
benefitting their lives and community.

It was a place of talk and planning;
sharing, sympathy and understanding.
Revolving words of weather and land;
help was always close at hand.

Exhausted with the harvest done,
banquets, dancing and visiting fun.
Dimming the past...lit by the future,
seasons rush with hope the suture.

# v. Old Houses

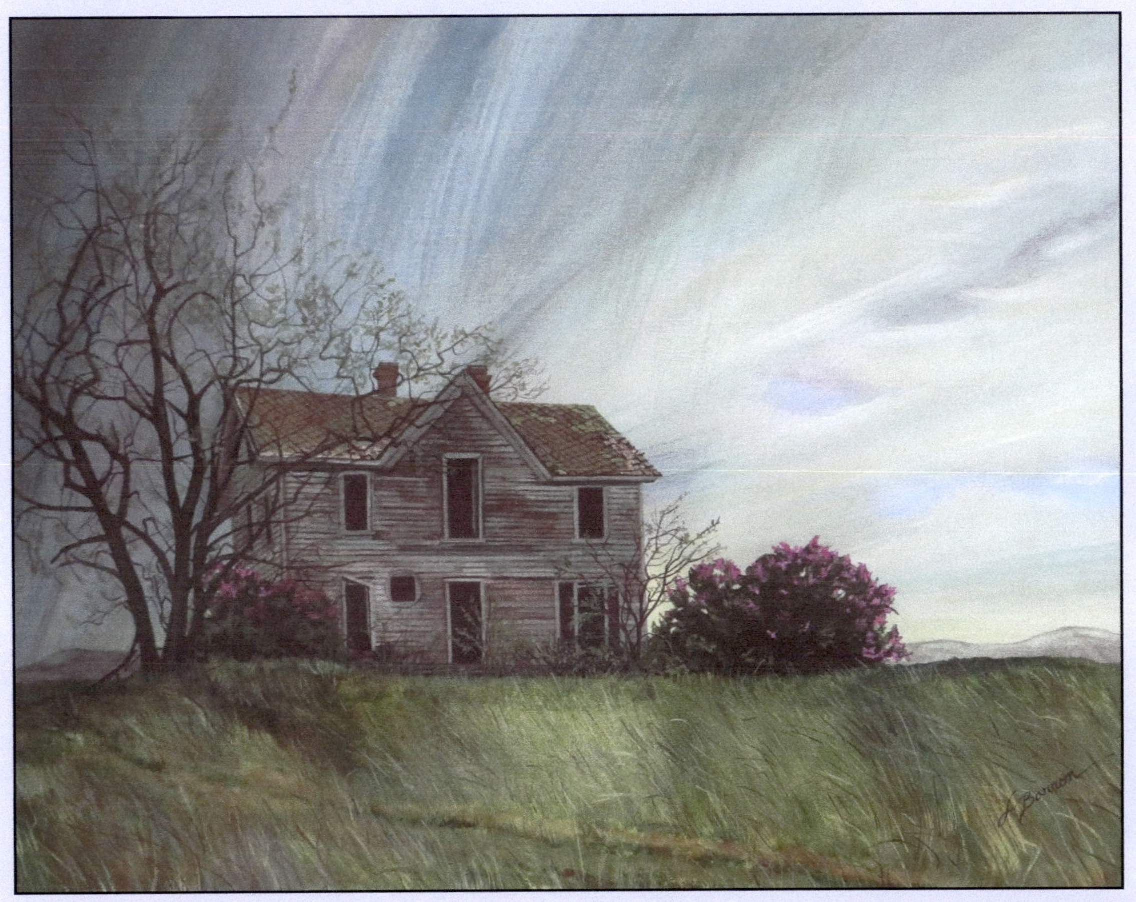

Approaching Rain

## Hollowed Spaces

In the lead, Father Time races
through deserted hollowed spaces.
Tiny bouquets droop from places,
now adorned with water stain faces.
Routine life by husband and wife;
absconded...all their joys and strife.
Nobody passes on creaky floor boards,
once tread upon by lasses and lords.
Faded the proud coat of paint;
broken china cup so quaint.
The barn once held sustaining grain;
moss roof lets in pouring rain.
Who once opened the hanging door?
Thought they rich or thought they poor?
Thought they happy or thought they sad?
Greetings... a respite with visitors glad.
Did someone hold their stories dear,
lived by ones now buried near?
Soon the walls will crumble
heralded by a thunder's rumble.
A gentle spring wind will blow,
and new flowers will begin to grow.

# Cabins

A cabin was a sheltering place.

Ponder on those who shared tight space.

*They made their beds,*
*and bowed their heads;*
*often worked in isolation,*
*knew life's joys and tribulation,*
*kept a Bible close at hand,*
*homemade clothing…nothing grand;*
*prized pocket-knife, heirloom platter;*
*low loft accessed by a ladder.*

They never drifted far away,

self-sufficient in their stay

near mountain, stream or hollow,

their folks before them,

their sons to follow.

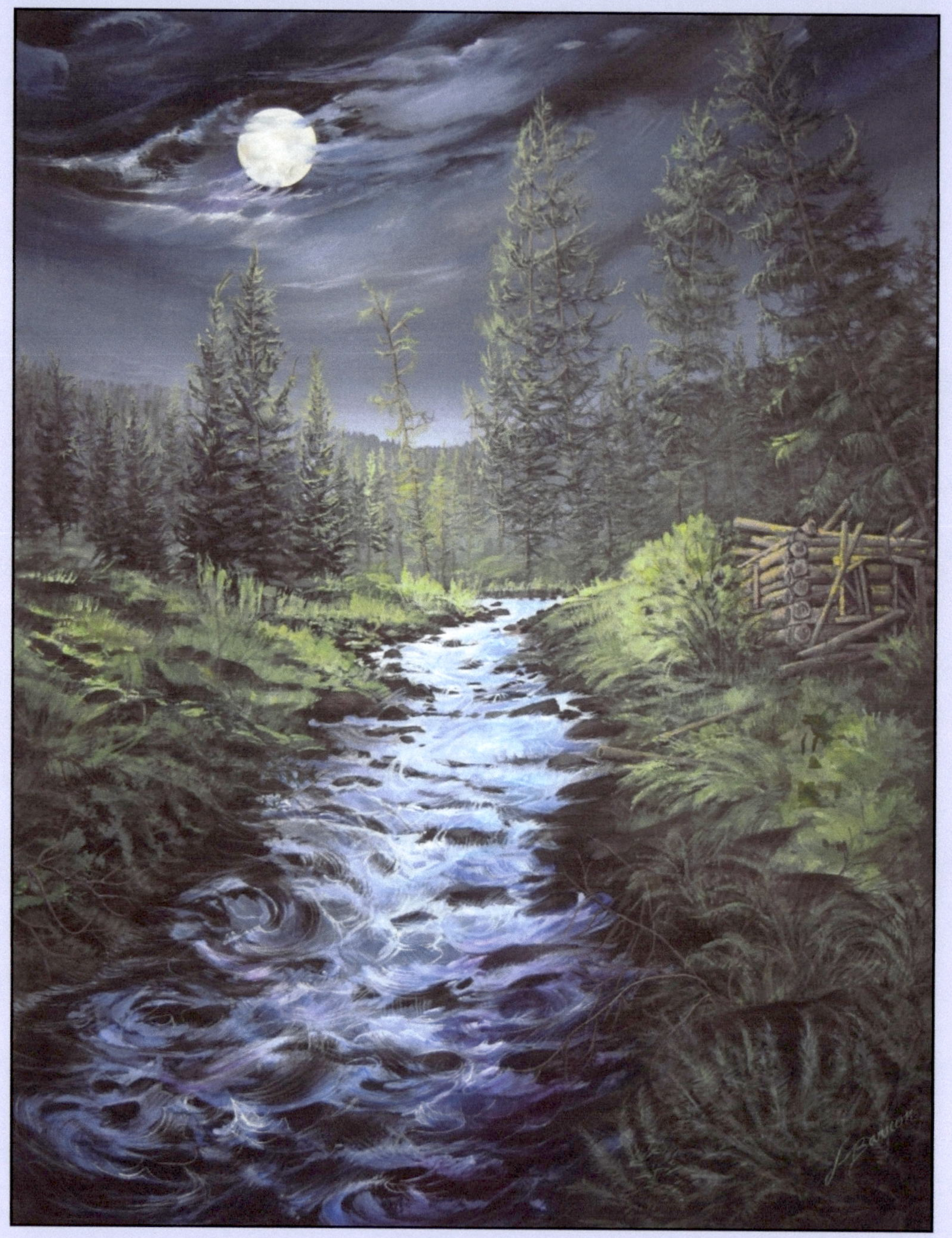

**Mountain Retreat**

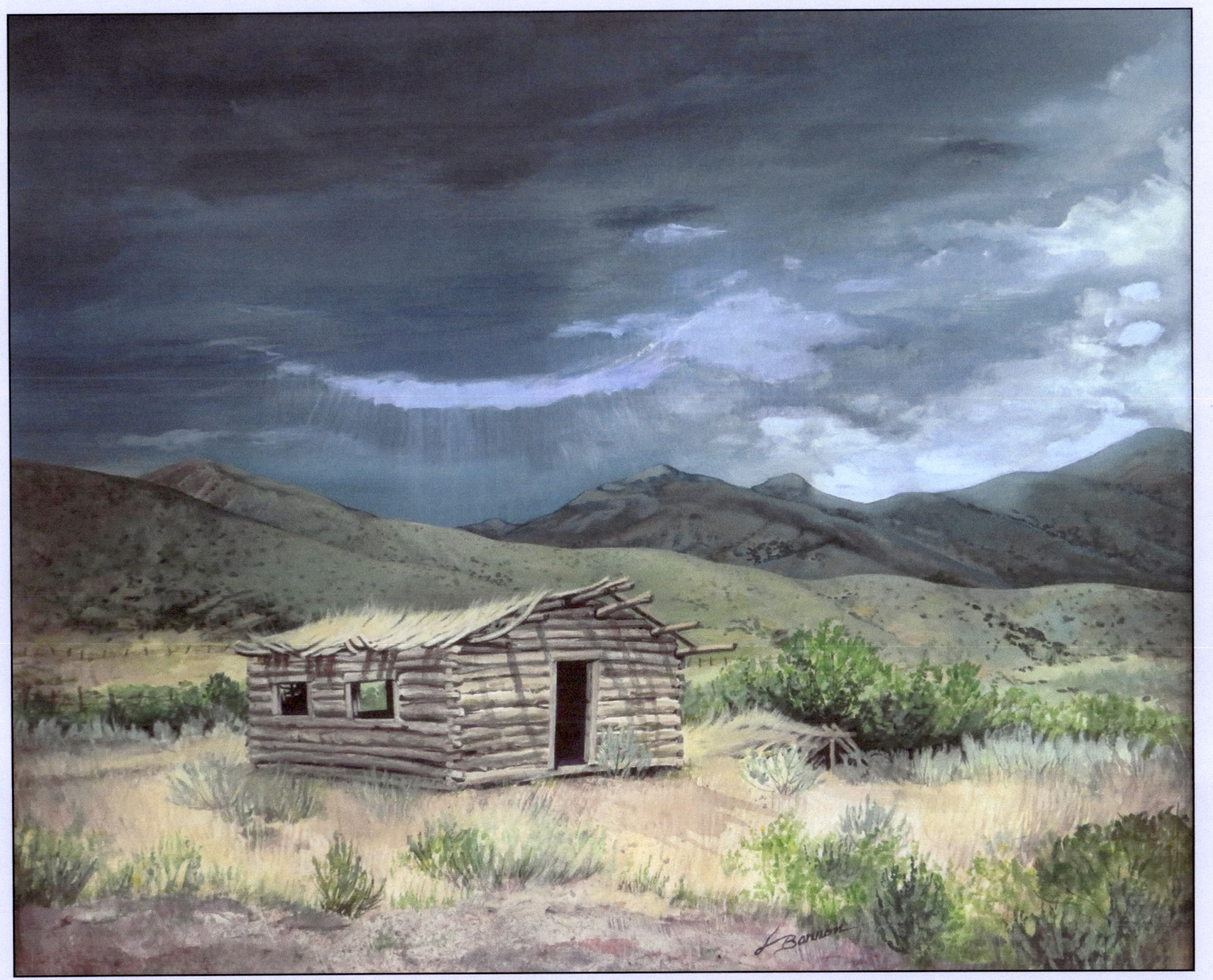

Smiling Down on Humble Abode II

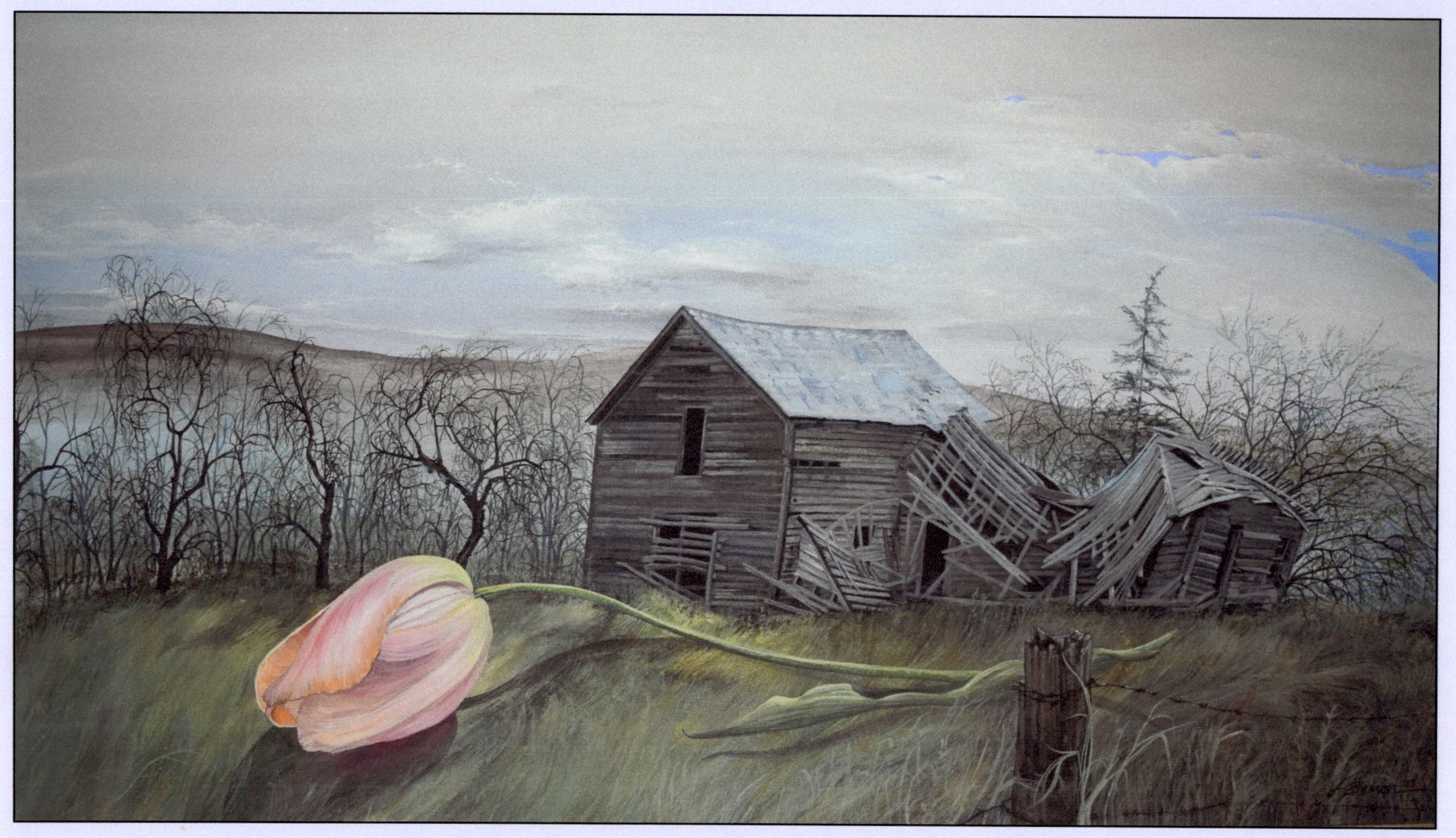

Renewal

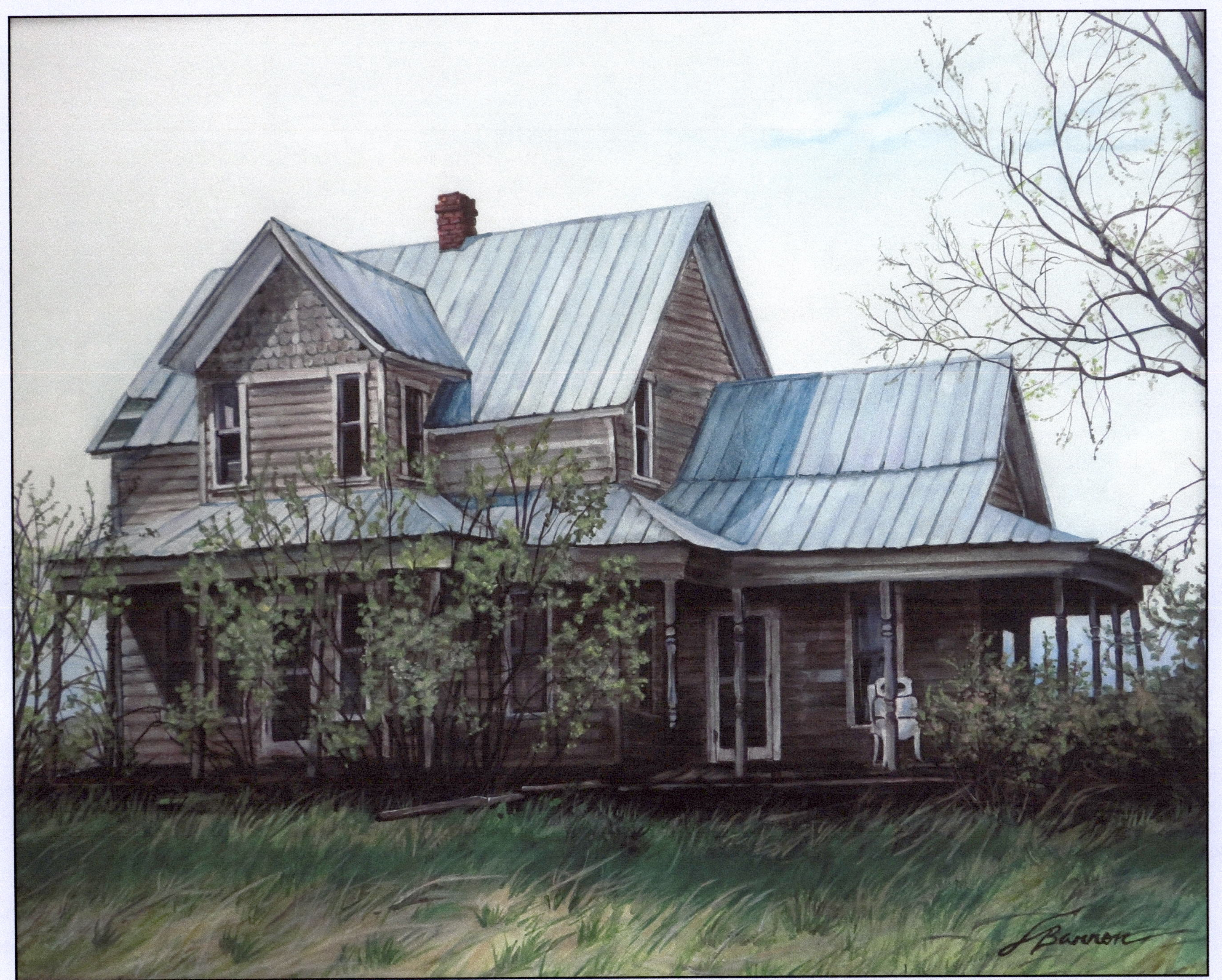

**No More Dirty Laundry**

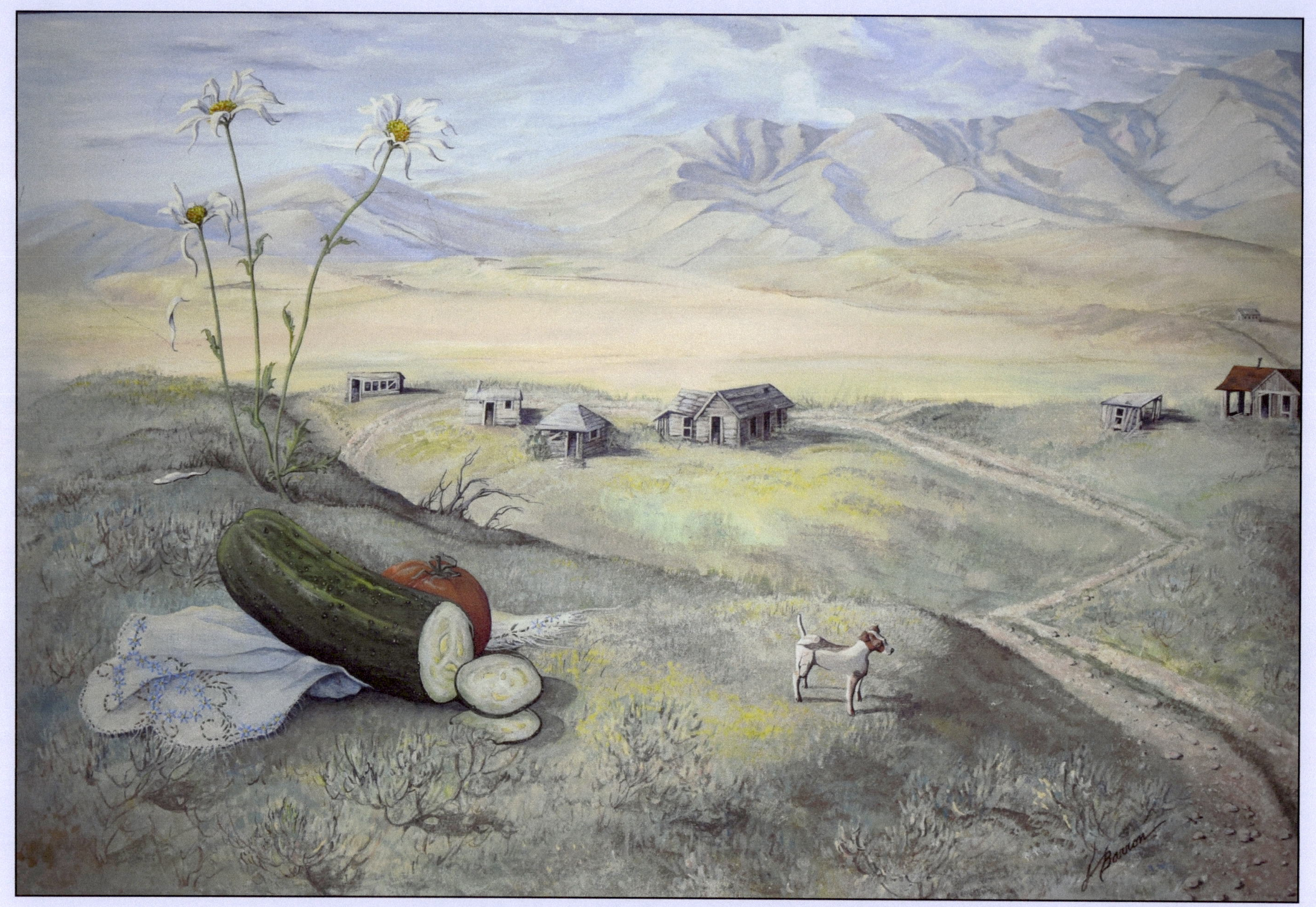

**Time Lassoed** | Gilmore, Idaho

# Gilmore, Idaho

Homes before the winter completed,

resources and strength depleted;

families to come along,

hoping to again belong.

Sharing in the weary wait;

wealth the promised bitten bait.

Silver torn from mountain shelter;

mule team wagons to the smelter.

In 1910 it burned to ground;

depleting mines closed all around.

The railroad came to heft ore load,

'til great depression saw all fold.

Boom now undeniably over,

people were replaced with clover.

Rails were pulled as last train left,

in its wake ... ghost town bereft.

Preservation's saving it from funk.

You can even buy a chunk.

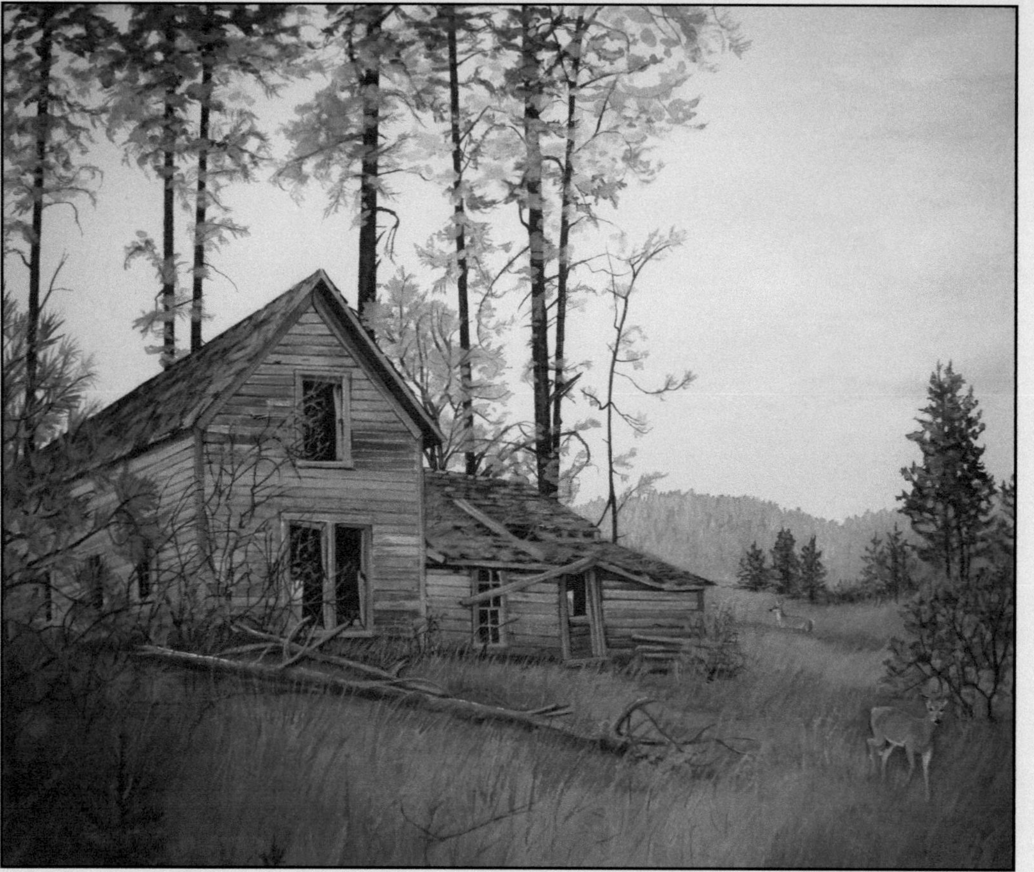


# Deserted House

There amongst the pines it hides,
caught on one of my back-road rides.
Drawn to it like dog to bone,
may my trespass stay unknown.
Feet crunch on the unkept ground,
birds announce with welcome sound.
Door is hanging off its hinges,
enter feeling reverent twinges.

Expectantly the smell is musty,
metal is rusty...surfaces dusty.
Clouded windows filter sun,
curtains closed when day was done.
Furnishing gratifyingly removed,
family members thus behooved.
Mottled walls that once embraced
celebrations...hardships faced.

Stories just a whisper blown...
blown into the great unknown.
Returning to the humble portal,
reminded of all things mortal,
flowers near the fencepost flourish,
faith and soil continue to nourish.
Behind the wheel I give a sigh,
"Thank you," as I wave goodbye.

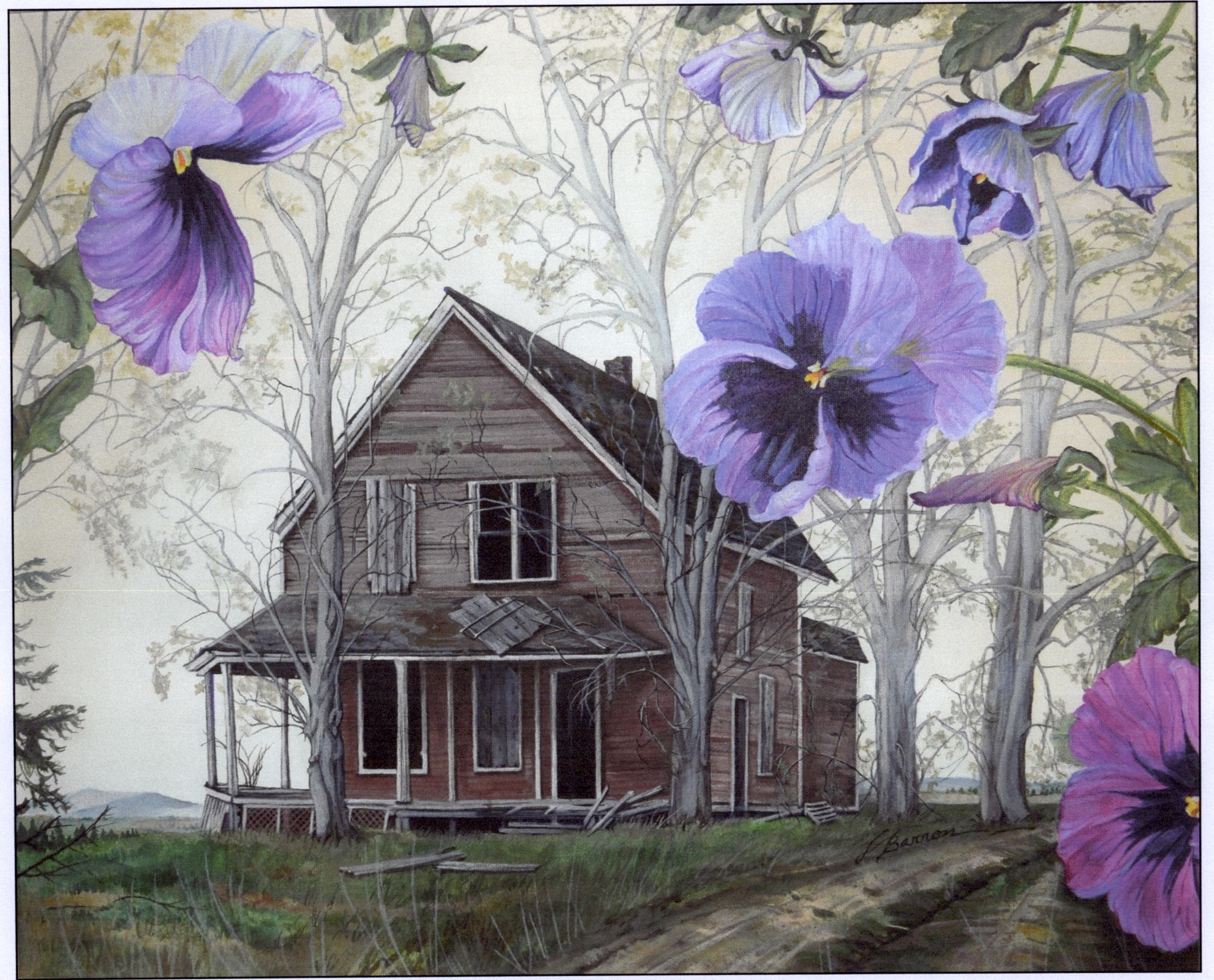

Cricket Song

# Estate Sale Dream

The covered porch was dark and huge.

I didn't crowd...not to seem rude.

The hordes weren't people, but on tables,

shelves, chairs and hanging from gables.

Fancies from a distance past

were being sold so they might last.

Treasured by aunts, sons and brothers,

and apparently by many others,

on dusty shelves were pushed and stacked,

grouped oddities ...some were cracked.

Atmosphere of a theatrical lair,

costumes, wigs and masks were there.

Not your average "junking" fare...

sugar cubes from Paris with care.

Foreign, bizarre intriguing stuff...

could stay hours...not get enough.

Fortunately, there was no rush;

my mouth fell in reverent hush.

Marionettes, vases and precious rocks,

staring dolls in hand knit socks,

tokens from country fairs and trips,

tools and guns held men in grips.

Jewelry like I'd never seen,

huge marbles...hanging lamps gave gleam.

Stained glass leaned on windowed wall,

pointing sign reads, *"more inside, see all."*

Great stacking toys and turtle shells,

stuffed animals and Indian bells.

My head rotated like a bobble;

*"More upstairs,"* steep steps to hobble.

Carved furniture haphazardly plopped,

so cluttered that it nearly dropped.

Old pottery, prints and Turkish rugs,

stacked linens, dishes and glassed-in bugs.

Endless things once held dear,

by people in photos no longer here.

Arms full as I went away,

smiling at this fun-filled day.

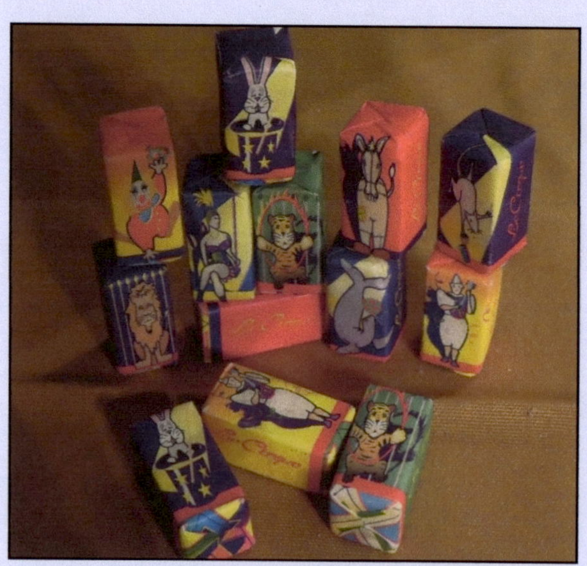

Wrapped sugar cubes (circus theme) were offered at our hotel.
I brought them home from Paris.

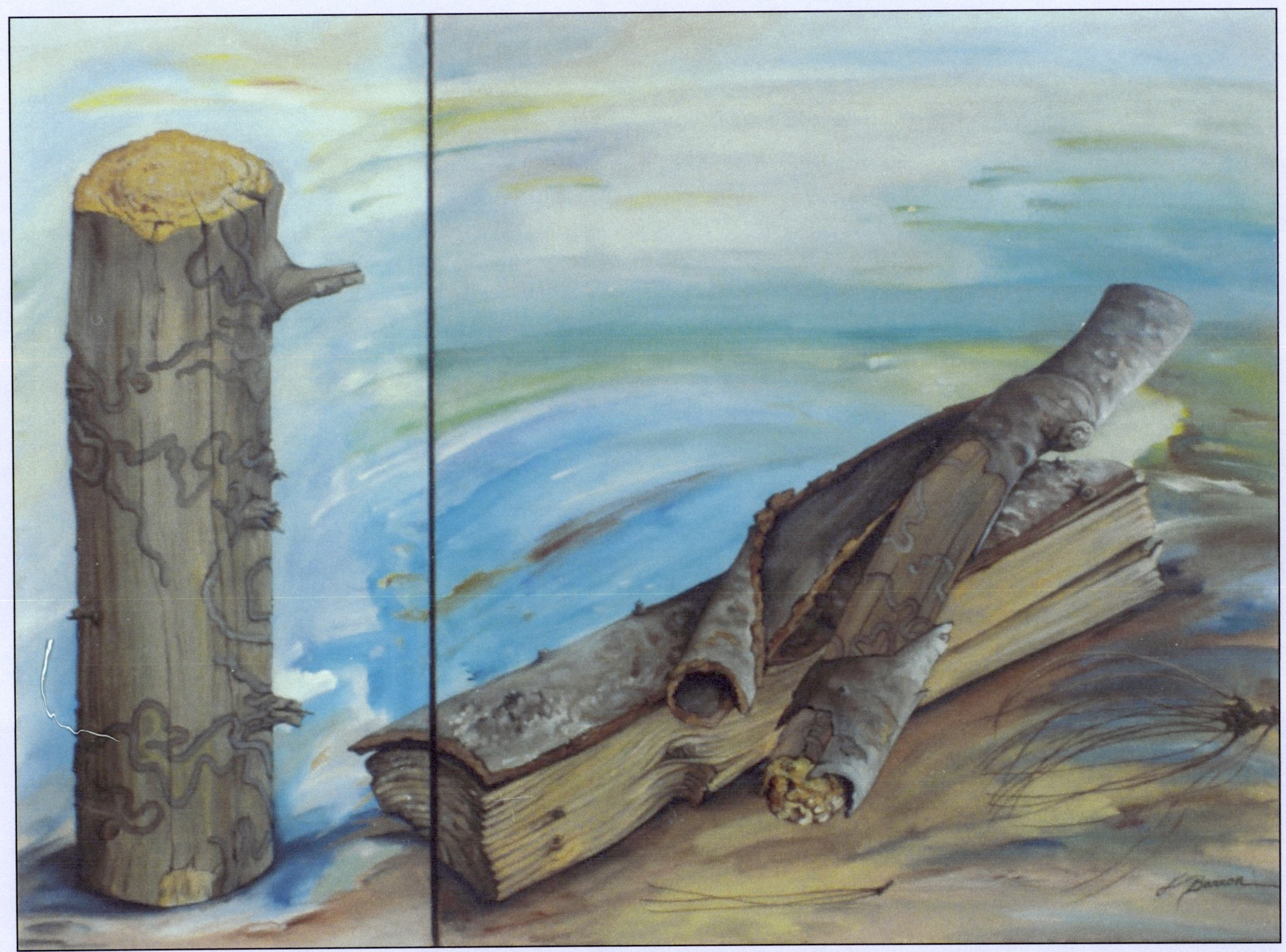

**Firewood Study** | diptych

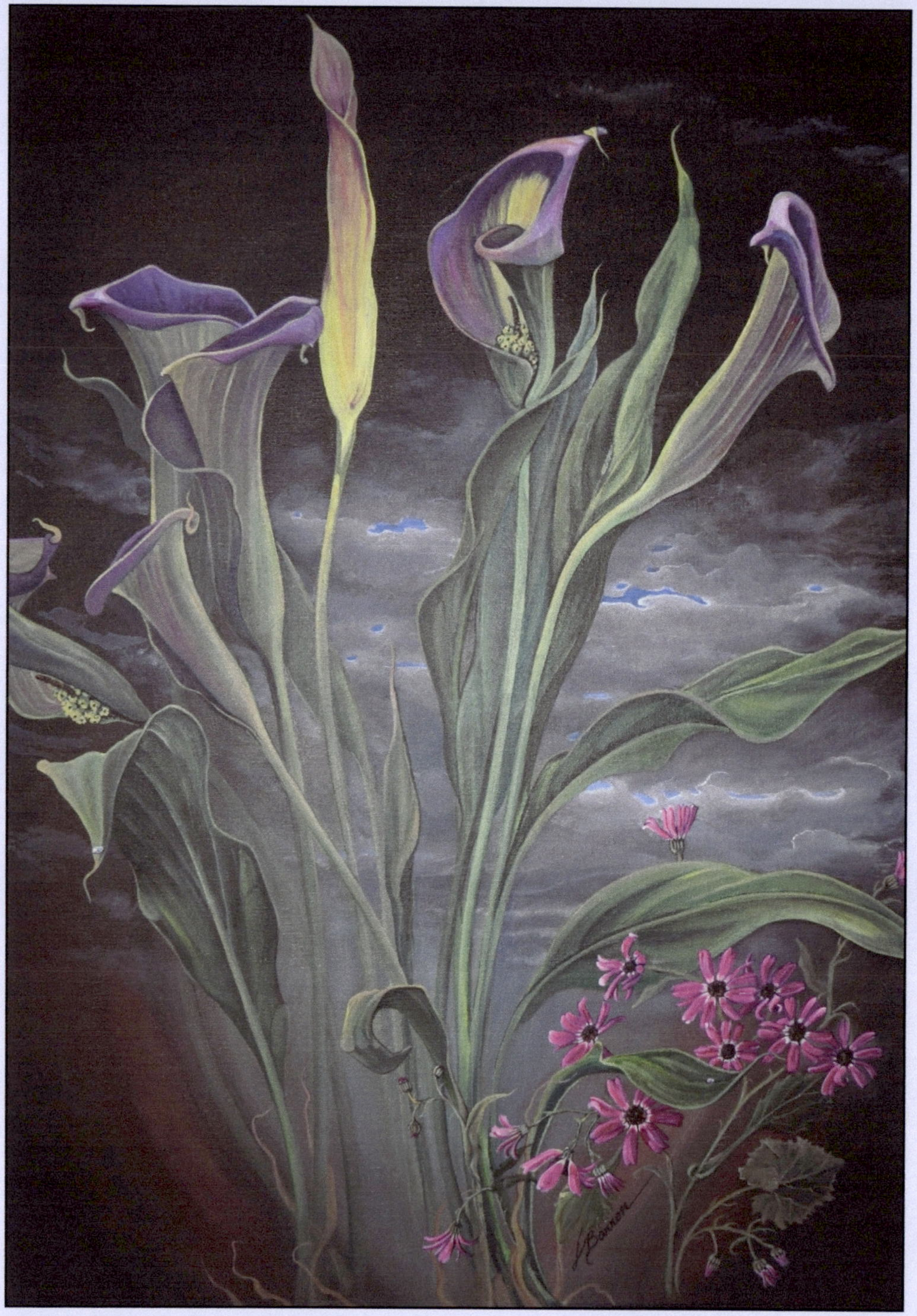

**Calla Lilies**

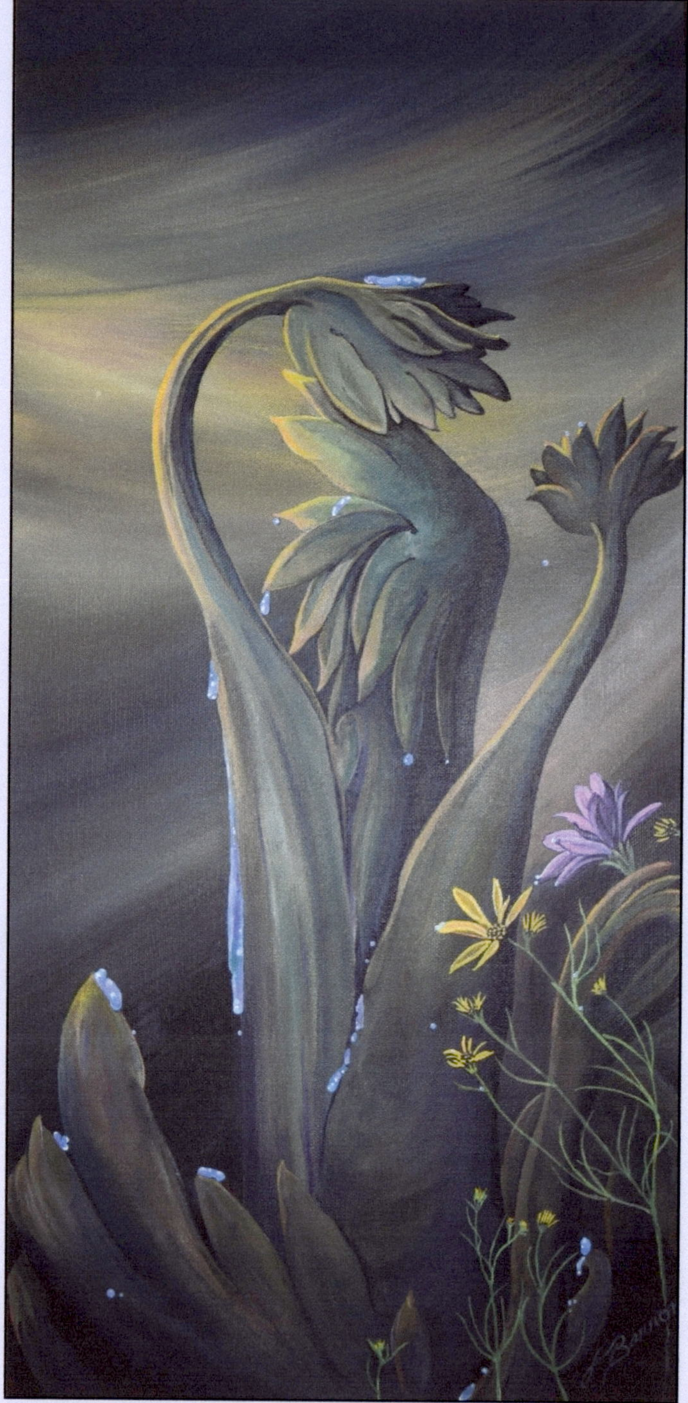

**Dual Nature** | at left a woman in a bonnet; at right a hooded executioner

# Flowers

Flowers toss the mood uplifted,
in field, garden, home or gifted.
Showmanship that pales the norm,
artistry of color and form;
intensity that dazzles eyes,
tiny or enormous size,
variety with place and seasons,
extravagant names for countless reasons:

*coreopsis, daffodil, bluebell, wisteria,
honeysuckle, tulip, lotus, petunia,
geranium, peony, fuchsia, begonia
snapdragon, carnation, pansy, dahlia,
sunflower, aster, foxglove, zinnia,
narcissus, hibiscus, hydrangea, magnolia,
lilac, delphinium, gladiola, viola.*

As they bloom beauty unfurls;
classic names for baby girls:

*Iris, Poppy, Heather, Lily,
Violet, Rose, Hyacinth, Daisy.*

Endless list if you're not lazy;
already you've been driven crazy?
Orchid, tulip or rose obsession,
kings brewed wars for sole possession.
Plant and tend them...in this caring,
it's a positive gift you're sharing.
From tubers or from seeds they're sown.
Their blossoms you can call your own,
as long as they are in your sight,
giving comfort, inspiration or delight.

## May you live with beauty.

*Diane Barron*